God's Addiction Recovery Plan

The Biblical Path to Freedom

Michael Wrenn

© 2018 by Michael Wrenn

All Scripture quotations, unless indicated, are taken from the New American Standard Bible Copyright © 1960, 1962, 1963, 1968, 1971, 1972, 1973, 1975, 1977, 1995 by The Lockman Foundation, La Habra, CA. Used by permission.

To my mother, who introduced me to the word of God and loved me despite my rebellion. Thanks to my wife, and mother-in-law who painstakingly assisted me with the editing process.

Contents

Preface

The problem of alcohol and drug addiction has reached epidemic proportions in the United States and around the world. Alcoholism runs rampant across the globe, drug abuse continues to consume its victims, and addiction to prescription drugs appears to be at an all-time high. Many rehabilitation facilities have waiting lists for admittance, detoxification centers abound, the morgue slabs are full, and funeral homes continue to profit on the crisis of addiction stalking both old and young alike. Is there an answer? Is there a remedy to this destructive force that has been unleashed upon our planet? Is there hope for those who suddenly awaken to discover their lives have been devastated and destroyed by addiction? Families are being decimated, the home is being ripped apart, prisons are filled to capacity, and Hollywood has seen its share of deaths. Darkness gloats over the millions who are destroyed by the ravages of this destructive plague. For many, if not most, the quest for recovery is a continual cycle of failure, a merry-go-round of treatment that is most often futile, empty and even useless in many cases. Hollywood constantly parades stars who find themselves in and out of jail, in treatment facilities and experiencing one marriage failure after another. Thousands of families are destroyed every year by problems associated with addiction.

Is there a genuine solution to the problem of addiction haunting the lives of millions? Is there a proven method or path an addict can follow to find complete recovery and never again return to a lifestyle of addiction? Is there an affordable means whereby the financially challenged can gain freedom and live to find a productive, meaningful and satisfying life in society? The answer is an absolute resounding yes! God has a proven track record throughout the history of mankind in making something beautiful out of those who have been marred, stained, defiled, broken and destroyed. He is the Master who specializes in changing lives, mending broken hearts, and putting back together the pieces of a wasted life. The Almighty has an answer for everything and addiction is no exception to the rule.

Most addiction recovery programs around the world require insurance or substantial financial resources to gain entrance, and many addicts simply do not have the monetary means of acquiring professional treatment. Many of those without financial means to acquire adequate help, find themselves in a vicious cycle of dependency, and fall back onto the path of destruction within hours, days or weeks of leaving a detoxification facility. All too often treatment centers are nothing more than revolving doors for those who have insurance or abundant financial resources to maintain a regular quest for sobriety. In many cases treatment is only a means or an attempt to escape the negative consequences of behavior, to escape judicial discipline or avoid jail time. Yes indeed, the addict is a master at playing the game.

God has provided man with a free addiction recovery program that only requires his acceptance, commitment, participation, diligence, perseverance and determination. The addict can be set free by the power of a loving God who longs to break the bonds and shackles of those enslaved to this monster. God will deliver those who look to Him and place their faith in the Lord Jesus Christ. The Bible indicates God can help. He has a solution for those who find themselves in the clutches of sin. God will deliver those who dare to put complete trust and confidence in Him. He is able to restore those who have been ravaged, cast down, set aside and deemed as being beyond redemption. Jesus Christ is a Master at repairing and restoring those captured by sin. He is the Great Physician who can rehabilitate those mangled by the destructive powers of darkness. God is well able to break the chains that bind and shackle the addict.

God's recovery plan will do for the addict what no standard treatment program or facility will ever aspire too. May you discover in God's Addiction Recovery Plan along The Biblical Path to Freedom, a power able to transform the lowest of the low. You can come to know, experience, and enjoy the life God has planned for you. The addict can be free from the one who "comes to steal and kill and destroy" (John 10:10). I pray you come to experience and understand the words of Jesus Christ when He said, "So if the Son makes you free, you will be free indeed" (John 8:36). Jesus came to set men free; "The

Son of God appeared for this purpose, to destroy the works of the devil" (1 John 3:8).

Addiction is one of the many works of the devil that Jesus came to conquer and overcome. Through the nightmare of addiction, evil seeks to destroy those who find themselves in its awful throws of torment. The addict can experience complete recovery by adhering to God's Addiction Recovery Plan and following The Biblical Path to Freedom.

Introduction

God's Addiction Recovery Plan is unlike the journey that most addiction recovery programs suggest, present, practice and teach. The Biblical Path to Freedom is unique because the world does not understand, nor can it know the ways and thoughts of God.

> Let the wicked forsake his way and the unrighteous man his thoughts; and let him return to the Lord, and He will have compassion on him, and to our God, For He will abundantly pardon. For My thoughts are not your thoughts, nor are your ways My ways, declares the Lord. For as the heavens are higher than the earth, so are My ways higher than your ways and My thoughts than your thoughts (Isaiah 55:7-9).

The world's ways and thoughts toward addiction will never measure up to God's understanding, knowledge, insight and wisdom on the subject of enslavement. God is the Creator of man, and fully knows why man behaves in certain ways. The Almighty understands the depths of man's depravity and corruption; therefore, He alone is able to provide man with the solution to his primary problem. God's plan of redemption and freedom for man has been clearly set forth in His manual for life. His plan for man can be summed up in what is one of the best-known verses of Scripture found in the word of God: "For God so loved the world, that He gave His only begotten Son, that whoever believes in Him shall not perish, but have eternal life" (John 3:16).

God has His own unique way of doing things. He has declared His way to us through His Son Jesus Christ and the written word of God. Man will never learn to think like God unless he undergoes a supernatural change and thereby is given the capacity to do so. In his sinful state, man is always seeking to do things his own way, rather than adhering to the ways, means and dictates of God. Secular recovery programs most often teach "once an addict always an addict," and "once an alcoholic always an alcoholic." To the contrary, the truth defined by the word of God teaches an individual can be transformed and become a new person. "Therefore, if anyone is in Christ, he is a new creature" (2 Corinthians 5:17). Through a supernatural transformation performed by receiving Jesus Christ as Lord and Savior, an individual can begin and experience a new life. This transformation takes place within the core of man's being, and in turn allows him to say, "I am no longer the person I once was; I have become a new creature in Christ." Secular addiction recovery programs offer the addict a process of reformation, while God's program offers man a spiritual transformation from within. This is an internal change which in turn affects his entire being in body, soul, and mind. Jesus Christ has the power to internally transform the human spirit. The individual who adheres to God's calling will become a new person, no longer in bondage to the old corrupted life. When God sets an addict free, he is no longer in bondage; no longer enslaved to alcohol, drugs, or anything else. God's Addiction Recovery Plan and The Biblical Path to Freedom confront addiction at the very root of the problem, a sinful nature.

God's word teaches that men and women are born as sinners. Man is corrupted and defiled in the womb at conception. The Psalmist wrote, "Behold, I was brought forth in iniquity, and in sin my mother conceived me" (Psalm 51:5). David is speaking of a sinful nature that was passed down by the first man Adam to all of his descendants. Sin brought the curse of spiritual and physical death upon man. The apostle Paul under inspiration of the Holy Spirit writes, "For all have sinned and fall short of the glory of God" (Romans 3:23). Long before any addict ever used, indulged in, or abused alcohol and drugs, God classified him as a sinner. Addiction is only a symptom of the root problem that leads men into a state of bondage to alcohol, drugs and other forms of captivity. If you can destroy the root of the problem, you can eliminate the effects and symptoms. No one ever becomes an addict by doing something only once. Addiction is the result of a continued choice to violate the word of God by living a lifestyle contrary to what God has commanded. The addict must recognize that his underlying problem is sin and disobedience. The effects of continued disobedience will lead man into a habitual lifestyle of sin. This in turn affects him physically, mentally, emotionally and spiritually.

The spiritual aspect of addiction recovery is the most important element of discovering and recovering from its effects. This is where the deadly root of the problem can be identified. The addict must place an emphasis upon the spiritual aspect of his quest for freedom, if he is to experience complete recovery. Most addiction programs emphasize the need for a spiritual program. At the same time, they fail to lead the addict to the only spiritual source who can adequately deal with the sin infestation that has led to his addiction. Jesus Christ is the only source who can deal with the sin that has infected everyone born into this world, and He offers the addict much more than remission from a disease. His promise is a new life, a new attitude, and a new foundation upon which to build. Man was created by God as a physical and spiritual being. The spiritual part of man is where God deals with and transforms the inner person. A man's spiritual heart or his core being is commonly referred to as his spirit in the Bible.

The Bible teaches that man is not just another creature grazing on the pastures of a plain. He is not just another animal. God's word describes man as being created in God's image and likeness. Then God said, "Let Us make man in Our image, according to Our likeness" (Genesis 1:26). This image and likeness in man was marred in his rebellion against God. It was contaminated when man turned against God in disobedience and insisted on partaking of the forbidden fruit. A physical abnormality can be passed down genetically from parents to their children. The same is true with regard to Adam who spiritually passed down the seed of sin to his children and all of their descendants who would follow. Adam's disobedience brought physical and spiritual death to the human race. Man is born a sinful creature, infected by sin's deadly venom that produces spiritual sickness in many forms, fashions and shapes. Sin will manifest itself in men through many different means and measures. For some, it reveals itself in the destructive bondage of addiction. God initiated a plan to restore man to the righteous state he lost in his rebellion. Adam's disobedience came as no surprise to God. Long before Adam sinned against God, the solution to the problem had already been provided. God would restore and reconcile Himself with those who would accept His means of restoration. God would one day sacrifice His own Son Jesus Christ as a payment for man's sin.

The problems that men experience today are either a direct result of their own rebellion, or indirectly the result of someone else's disobedience. Jesus Christ is God's restorative plan. In His word, God makes it clear that no other means of salvation and deliverance from sin's deadly consequences is available. There is no other way to acquire a right relationship with God, and no other means of acquiring true freedom from the bondage and penalty of sin. Jesus said, "I came that they might have life, and have it abundantly" (John 10:10). The life of an addict is everything but abundant living. The destructive nature of addiction is the complete opposite of fulfillment, contentment and satisfaction. Jesus Christ described and defined Himself as "the way, and the truth, and the life" (John 14:6). There is no existing life outside of Jesus Christ. Every individual without Him is defined as spiritually dead. Notice what Paul says in his letter to the Colossians about Jesus Christ and who He is with regard to the purposes of God.

> He is the image of the invisible God, the first-born of all creation. For by Him all things were created, both in the heavens and on earth, visible and invisible, whether thrones or dominions or rulers or authorities, all things have been created through Him and for Him (Colossians 1:15,16).

Until a man discovers life in Jesus Christ and submits to Him as his Creator, he is essentially a walking dead man. He physically exists, but has no spiritual life within to produce fulfillment, peace and joy. His life is filled with a multitude of mistakes, miscalculations, bad decisions and poor choices. He is plagued by the curse and penalty of God's Law. In his sinful state, he will never be what God desires. Addicts spend a lifetime making poor decisions and mistakes. If the addict is to experience true freedom from addiction, he must begin to make sound decisions and right choices on a regular basis. Looking to Christ is the first wise choice and the best decision in life anyone will ever make. Receiving Jesus Christ as one's personal Lord and Savior is the first step in discovering the wonderful plan that God has designed for those who will place their confidence and trust in Him. He is the first step to experiencing deliverance from a lifestyle of habitual sin. Only He can provide a life of victory, peace, joy, contentment, fulfillment and righteousness.

The purpose of this book is to help the addict discover a new life in Jesus Christ and inform others as to the real truth about addiction. Victory and deliverance are available to all who will simply call upon Him and place their lives under His management. "And it shall be that everyone who calls on the name of the Lord will be saved" (Acts 2:21). Salvation is available to all who will take a leap of faith by calling on the Lord Jesus Christ for redemption and deliverance. Once a person has made this necessary and important decision, he will discover what the Apostle Paul meant when he wrote, "I can do all things through Him who strengthens me" (Philippians 4:13). God earnestly desires to deliver man from the bondage of his addiction. He longs to redeem and deliver the addict who finds himself enslaved to alcohol, drugs, or any other means of bondage. The Lord earnestly desires for man to experience spiritual freedom. He longs for man to be content, fulfilled, satisfied, and blessed with the precious gift of spiritual life. Receiving God's gift of eternal life is the entrance way to receiving all He has to offer.

Eternal life can be defined as both qualitative and quantitative; it is everlasting life and much more. God has a beautiful and glorious plan for each of those who choose to submit their lives to Him. He requires a simple commitment to obedience in walking with Him through all of life's situations and circumstances. True life is found in discovering God's purpose for our lives, and then placing that plan into action as He directs. Man's responsibility involves right choices, obeying God, and making proper decisions. As man chooses to make the right choice and obey God rather than following after worldly pleasures, life will progress into abundant living, contentment, peace, joy, and fulfillment.

The word of God has made it abundantly clear regarding God's revelation to man. "You will seek Me and find Me when you search for Me with all your heart" (Jeremiah 29:13). The addict desiring complete recovery would do well to seek God with the same tenacity as which he has sought after the pleasures and desires of the world. He will need to commit the time he has spent indulging in alcohol, drugs, and other fleshly appetites, to seeking after the Lord. A diligent quest for God cannot be a part time effort; it requires all of one's energies. The recovering addict must learn to eat, breathe and sleep Jesus Christ who will serve to replace the alcohol, drugs, and sinful indulgences of the flesh. He will need to forsake his sin and become addicted to Christ. The requisite for seeking God with all of one's heart is to dethrone self and place

Christ at the center of one's life. Jesus Christ must become everything to the man or woman who would choose to seek after Him with all their heart. Man must allow God to consume his passions, ambitions, dreams and desires. Here is where the addict will find true freedom from the addiction plaguing and tormenting his soul. Most addicts continue in their lifestyle of bondage because they have no other reason or purpose to live. Addiction has permeated their way of living; therefore, they live as if there is no other alternative.

Change requires a permanent decision to turn around. The addict needs to accept God's way as the only right way. He may then move forward in the proper direction by determining with all of his heart to be obedient to the word of God. Addicts travel a road that could rightly be defined as Torment Alley. It's never a pleasant path, not an exciting journey, and certainly not an enjoyable adventure. Addiction is a life filled with sorrow, pain, misery, heartache, suffering, disappointment, chaos and depravity. The only path and means of freedom is to turn around and head in the opposite direction. The addict must recognize he is traveling in the wrong direction. He must come to see that he is traveling a path in opposition to the defined way of God. The active addict is traveling in a direction which is hostile and displeasing to his Creator.

The addict must recognize the root of his addiction is sin. His problem is self and the choice to continue living in darkness. Jesus said, "This is the judgment, that Light has come into the world, and men loved darkness rather than the light, for their deeds were evil" (John 3:19). The addict's problem is not someone or something else as he is so often prone to point the finger at. The addict's greatest problem is himself, and the sin that has taken him captive. He must make a conscious decision to turn from himself, turn from his sin, and turn to Jesus Christ by faith. This is where the addict will receive change, begin a new life of sobriety and discover the victory of recovery. Only upon making such a vital decision to turn around will the addict begin a new journey toward a victorious, peaceful, joyful and righteous life.

Anything or anyone threatening an individual's allegiance and commitment to God must be forsaken. It all begins with recognizing the problem of sin. The addict's real enemy is a devilish nature causing him to be involved in various measures of darkness. Problems not recognized, cannot and will not be resolved. All addiction programs teach that an addict must recognize and accept the existence of a problem before he will seek a solution and come to resolve. This fact is also resonated in God's Addiction Recovery Plan. The addict must take personal responsibility for his sinful actions. Those in bondage are well known for the tendency to point the finger of blame at someone else. Until an addict recognizes he has a problem and that he is the culprit, he will not seek help and resolve.

What is the real problem embedded deep within the depths of the addict's soul? Most addiction recovery programs provide answers based upon philosophy, psychology, sociology and psychiatry. God's Addiction Recovery Plan defines the root of addiction as a very specific problem known as sin. Once an addict recognizes his addiction is due solely to a continued choice to persist in disobedience to God by yielding to his sin nature, he may then set out to remedy the problem that has enslaved and held him captive. God has blessed man with one remedy to resolve the sin issue; the sacrifice of His Son Jesus Christ on the cross. Through the death of Jesus Christ and the "power of His resurrection" (Philippians 3:10) indwelling the believer, the addict can discover a new life worth living without alcohol or drugs. Being high on Jesus is an internal experience that is free of charge. It is a much greater high than can ever be induced and experienced by a substance. Jesus made a great promise to those who would truly look to Him, obey Him, and receive Him by faith.

> Now on the last day, the great day of the feast, Jesus stood and cried out saying, "if anyone is thirsty, let him come to Me and drink. He who believes in Me, as the Scripture said, from his innermost being will flow rivers of living water" (John 7:37-38).

Jesus offers His followers a well of life that never runs dry. He offers drink that will meet and fulfill the deepest need of man's innermost being. God will supply the well and fill it as needed. This is spiritual drink that delivers and sets captives such as the addict free. Speaking to the Samaritan woman as she came to draw water from a well, Jesus said to her, "Everyone who drinks of this water will thirst again; but whoever drinks of the water that I will give him shall never thirst; but the water that I will give him will become in him a well of water springing up to eternal life" (John 4:13-14). This was a woman who had lived her life in sin. She was guilty of drinking from the unfulfilling wells of the world. The addict is guilty of drinking from polluted and poisoned wells that saturate and fill his mind with stinky thinking. He somehow believes his drug of choice will eventually satisfy the need and cry of his human heart. Only the pure water flowing from the living well of God's grace and mercy will ever satisfy the true longings of man. God's well of life will replace the putrid waters of the world of which an addict finds himself continually drinking.

The Biblical Path to Freedom does not promise a problem free life. God never promises anyone a life void of trouble. He does promise to see His people through whatever they are confronted with. Many addict's spend years creating problems that will not suddenly disappear. Coming to Christ is not an immediate and instant cure all. God is greater than any problem the child of God will ever encounter. His word gives a special assurance to those who place their trust and confidence in Him. "God causes all things to work together for good to those who love God, to those who are called according to His purpose" (Romans 8:28). This promise would include the past, present, and future of those who look to Jesus Christ by faith in receiving Him as Lord and Savior. God never promises a road free of potholes. To the contrary, He indicates man will face trials, temptations and tribulations throughout his earthly sojourn. The great promise of God is that He will see His children through whatever problems arise. I pray God will use this book to point you in the direction of a life that will be filled with contentment, peace, joy and righteousness.

There is no other path to freedom than the one provided by God in Jesus Christ. God's plan is discovered in His written word. He has revealed Himself to us through His Son. Jesus said He was "sent to proclaim release to the captives, and recovery of sight to the blind, to set free those who are oppressed" (Luke 4:18). To be bound by addiction is to be held captive, to be oppressed and blinded to the reality of a better way. The addict who truly turns to Christ will discover truth in Him, and in turn find a life worth living. It is a glorious life of purpose, meaning, fulfillment, peace, joy and victory. It can be yours when you look to the Creator of all that is and all that ever will be.

I have personally completed God's Addiction Recovery Plan and traveled the difficult path of recovery. I discovered through personal experience that the path of addiction, rebellion and disobedience is one of the most difficult roads an individual can choose to follow. I understand what it means to "enjoy the passing pleasures of sin" (Hebrews 11:25). At the same time, I understand those temporary pleasures will lead to a bitter and remorseful end. How eloquently did Solomon describe such a life in his writings?

> Who has woe? Who has sorrow? Who has strife? Who has complaints? Who has needless bruises? Who has bloodshot eyes? Those who linger over wine, who go to sample bowls of mixed wine. Do not gaze at wine when it is red, when it sparkles in the cup, when it goes down smoothly! In the end it bites like a snake and poisons like a viper (Proverbs 23:29-32).

The preceding Scripture aptly applies to those who have become addicted to alcohol or drugs. It is tantamount to a living torment on earth. I have experienced the loneliness, heartache, misery, pain and suffering that addiction brings and imposes upon its captives. I have followed God's Addiction Recovery Plan and traveled The Biblical Path to Freedom. I have discovered a life filled with the joy of knowing the One and Only True God; a life filled with meaning, purpose, peace, fulfillment and contentment. It is a glorious life promising to extend and increase into eternity. God has prepared a home in an eternal kingdom, and promises to one day erase all suffering, heartache, misery, pain and loneliness. I pray you may discover and experience The Biblical Path to Freedom for yourself. Solomon in his wisdom wrote, "Good understanding gives favor: but the way of transgressors is hard" (Proverbs 13:15 KJV).

Addiction is a difficult way of life, haunting and driving its victims to utter despair day by day. Understanding and acting upon truth will set the addict free from a life of despair and despondency. In chapter one I have written about my personal journey from addiction to freedom. May this testimony promote and plant a seed of hope in your heart, reveal to you a better way, and provide you with a clear course to follow. This is God's way of dealing with and confronting the issues, rather than turning to alcohol, drugs, or any other type of addictive behavior. God's Addiction Recovery Plan will work for anyone who has a bondage problem. The addict must determine to follow through in giving all of his heart, soul, and mind to the Creator who has designed and given him life.

At the time of this writing, I have over thirty years of sobriety. God's Addiction Recovery Plan is based upon thirty years of biblical study, working with other addicts, and personal experience in recovery. The Biblical Path to Freedom is the path I traveled in finding the victory that is available to all who would truly follow it. God will set the addict free, if he will truly turn to Christ with a sincere heart of repentance and desire for recovery. God cannot fail when we give Him the freedom to manage our lives by denying our own will and accepting His.

I have included my personal testimony for your encouragement. No one is beyond the ability of God's Addiction Recovery Plan to help. Each of the ten chapters following the personal testimony will be based upon ten steps to freedom. These ten steps are those I followed in my quest for victory over addiction.

Chapter 1

A Personal Testimony

I had lived the life of an addict for nearly ten years when Jesus Christ set me free from its daily nightmare. The resurrection power of Christ is greater than any weakness, habit, or sin plaguing man. Unable to free myself, I humbly asked God for deliverance, made a promise, and followed up with my commitment to Him. He would require me to forsake the world and all it offered. I would submit to His will and diligently pursue truth with all my heart, mind, and soul. I had to abandon my own life, desires and ambitions for His will. I came to realize I was "bought with a price" (1 Corinthians 6:20). I would be willing to accept whatever cross He would call me to bear and I delightfully carry it today. What the world thinks is of no longer any concern to me, I am called to please God, not the world.

No addict is beyond God's redemptive, saving, delivering power. God is never the problem. In his refusal to yield complete control to God, forsake self, and give up the world, man creates his own failures, digs his own holes, creates his own darkness and destroys himself.

At twenty-five years of age I had been through three rehabilitation programs for drug and alcohol addiction. My life was a miserable wreck, a total loss, and medical professionals had given me little hope of recovery. This is a brief story of the sinful lifestyle and a miraculous deliverance from the bondage holding me captive.

I was introduced to the Bible and Jesus Christ at the age of ten. As a child, I invited Jesus Christ into my life. Entering my teenage years, I rebelled against the truth and turned toward fulfilling the sinful desires of the flesh. This was the beginning of a ten-year adventure into the dark world of alcoholism, drug addiction, gambling and sexual promiscuity.

Upon graduation from high school, I enlisted in the United States Air Force. A military tour in the Philippines fueled the flame of sinful desire raging within the heart of my youth. Life was one party after another, centering on having a good time and living in the fast lane. It was a lifestyle which would eventually create conflict with military authorities. I entered my first addiction treatment facility as a twenty- year old at Clark Air Base in the Philippines. This was only an attempt to appease superiors and save my military career. I was living what I thought to be the good life, having a great time, and "enjoying the pleasures of sin for a season" (Hebrews 11:25 KJV). I had no intention of leaving the party and denying my fleshly appetites.

Three years later I would enter a second rehabilitation facility at Eglin Air Force Base in Florida. At this stage of my addiction, life had become a mere miserable existence. The end of the road seemed to be closing in with no light at the end of the tunnel. The party lifestyle of habitually chasing after the pleasures of the world had taken its toll. I lived for another high, another drunk, always seeking and searching for one more good time. Bound by the ravages of alcoholism and drug addiction, there appeared to be no escape. The anger, bitterness, hurt, pain, sorrow, loneliness and resentment drove me deeper into a life of despair. Continuing to revel in sin, I would soon be confronted with the option of voluntary resignation from the military, or face a court martial for failure to rehabilitate.

As a stipulation of my discharge agreement, I would enter a third recovery program at the age of twenty-five. The medical professionals at Veteran's Hospital in Hampton, Virginia, wrote in my medical records; "there is little hope for recovery." I would eat, drink, smoke, or snort anything in an attempt to experience and maintain another high. Speed, cocaine, LSD, valium, Quaaludes, hashish, alcohol and marijuana were in control. I had contributed to the destruction of a marriage and destroyed other personal relationships along this path of ruin. My military career was finished, and I was left with a few clothes and some miscellaneous items. Life had become unbearable and there seemed to be little reason to continue living. Eventually, I came to recognize God was my only hope of survival and recovery. Three rehabilitation facilities, visits with psychologists and psychiatrists had failed to repair the consequences of my sin. I was at the end of the road and a total wreck. My life had been shattered and broken into a thousand pieces. I had prayed and diligently sought God, while rapidly reaching a point of giving up any hope of recovery.

What would eventually prove to be the ultimate answer and victory was a spiritual seed that had been planted in my heart at the tender age of ten. Recovery would come as a result of this seed of hope in the God I had been introduced to as a child. On the brink of suicide, I made a desperate plea to Jesus Christ for deliverance from the addiction that brought destruction upon my mental, emotional, physical, and spiritual health. I took a good look at myself in the mirror and came to understand I had brought all this misery and woe upon myself. There was no one else to blame!

In humble prayer I acknowledged to God my hopelessness, despair and unbelief, while asking Him to make His presence known and provide me deliverance from this life of darkness. I pleaded with God to restore a vessel that had followed the wrong path and was reaping the whirlwinds of pain. I accepted full responsibility and accountability for my own actions, while understanding I had brought this upon myself in living a sinful lifestyle. I promised to completely surrender and commit my life to God without reservation. I determined to no longer be the master of my own destiny; I would utterly surrender my own will, ambitions, dreams and desires to the will of God. I was sincerely seeking and asking God for help. My determination was to make a complete surrender to the sovereign will and plan of God as He would lead, guide, instruct and counsel.

This same evening, I had a dream that has remained fixed in my mind throughout the years. In this dream I was taken back to my childhood and found myself standing in the backyard of my grandmother's home. This was a favorite place of refuge during my childhood years. In the dream, I stood as a child looking toward heaven. I watched as clouds appeared and rolled across the sky. Palm branches were darting across the heavens, and as I watched, they turned into doves. Continuing to look toward heaven, I watched as a man came down with his hands extended toward me. As the man approached, I lifted my hands toward him; our hands met and gripped one another. The man who came down from heaven lifted me slightly off the ground and immediately returned me to my grandmother's backyard. I then turned and stepped into the back porch of my grandmother's home, where I immediately noticed an old man on the floor who was dead and the appearance of bodily corruption was evident.

This man was a miserable wretch to look upon. Staring at the appearance of the old man brought the dream to its conclusion. I do not claim this to have been a vision, nor do I claim to have seen Jesus Christ. This was a very unusual dream that came to have personal meaning, and due to its vividness, I have never forgotten it.

Several months later Jesus Christ would miraculously deliver me from drug and alcohol addiction. The deliverance was miraculous to the extent that I was finally free and knew it. Joy, peace, and victory were the result of a glorious deliverance from that which almost succeeded in destroying me. Because of the vivid nature of this dream, it continued to weigh heavy upon my mind.

Many theologians refuse to believe the Spirit of God would minister to someone in dream today. I have found nothing in the word God that would forbid Him to minister to someone in this way personally, should He choose to do so. As a minister and believer of God's word, I do not believe God speaks to people in dreams on a regular basis as a means of communication, and one should be extremely careful with this issue. I do not claim to have received any new revelation beyond what is already written in the Scripture. This dream has remained vivid in my mind for over thirty years. I believe God personally ministered to my particular need, heart, situation and circumstance. This is what I have gleaned and believed over the years regarding the dream.

At the age of ten, I had invited Jesus Christ into my life to be my personal Lord and Savior. To this very day I can remember sitting in a church pew as the Spirit of God ministered to my heart through a message which brought tear inducing conviction. I can remember where I was sitting when I arose, walked the church aisle, and prayed with pastor
J.C. Brooks to receive Jesus Christ. I also followed up in obedience with water baptism as directed by Scripture.

It was as a child around the age of ten that I appeared to be in this dream. I believe the significance here is that I met Jesus Christ and was introduced to Him as a child. I believe the palm branches seen in the dream were symbolic of the victory over sin I so desperately needed and the doves represented the peace I was diligently pursuing. I believe the man who came down from heaven was representative of Jesus Christ who is depicted in the gospel of

John, "For the bread of God is that which comes down out of heaven, and gives life to the world" (John 6:33). I believe the old man on the floor of my grandmother's home is depicted in Paul's letter to the Ephesians.

> If indeed you have heard Him and have been taught by Him, as the truth is in Jesus, that you put off the old man which is corrupt according to the deceitful lust and be renewed in the spirit of your mind, and put on the new man, which after God is created in righteousness and true holiness (Ephesians 4:21 KJV).

The man who came down from heaven had lifted me up slightly off the ground and immediately set me back down? At this time in my life, I had been contemplating suicide, ready to end it all. I had cried out and prayed to God, asking Him to save my life from destruction and ruin. I now understand that God was not yet ready for me in heaven. Months later I would be called to preach the gospel and share the good news of Jesus Christ. I would be left on this planet to go and proclaim the good news that Jesus saves and delivers from sin. I would remain in my earthly sojourn for the express purpose of sharing hope with others who find themselves in the snares of despair, pain, misery and addiction.

At a point of total desperation in life, I had pleaded for the reality of Christ and made a request for God to make His presence known. I believe this is what the Holy Spirit has spoken to my heart over the years regarding the dream. Jesus Christ left His home in heaven over two thousand years ago and died for my sin, as He did for the "sin of the world" (John 1:29). When Jesus Christ came to earth as God in human flesh, He revealed Himself to all of mankind. When the Holy Spirit convicted my heart of sin as a child, God made His presence personally known to me. Once again, He made Himself very real to me in this dream. Throughout the years God has continued to be very real and present with me. In various ways He has proven His revelation in Jesus Christ to be true. He has likewise made Himself known to multitudes of others who have accepted Him as their personal Lord and Savior.

In the months following this dream, Jesus Christ miraculously delivered me from the nightmare of drug and alcohol addiction with a mighty hand. A small glimpse of God's glory changed my life forever, when I truly realized who

Jesus Christ was, who I was in Him, and what He had done for me. As I once watched sin progressively seek to destroy my life, I have watched God restore and renew it. He has blessed me and brought about complete recovery from addiction. The victory over sin I longed for was discovered and found in Jesus Christ. I now understand and possess "the peace of God, which surpasses all comprehension" (Philippians 4:7). This peace resides deep within my heart and mind. I have experienced the joy provided in a meaningful and personal relationship with the Creator.

I have a meaningful and purposeful life in Christ that takes me to bed in peace each evening, and awakens me every morning to a new, glorious, and exciting day. As each day passes, I experience a greater appreciation and love of life. Above all else, the inner reality of eternal life has destroyed the old man who once produced misery, woe and pain. God has brought to surface the resurrected spiritual man who yearns and desires to walk with God. What Jesus Christ has done for me, He has done for multitudes of others. He will do the same for anyone who sincerely cries out to Him for salvation and deliverance. Jesus Christ longs for you to invite Him into your life as Lord and Savior. He yearns to meet the genuine desires and needs of your heart. He desires to give you a fruitful, productive, meaningful, and joyful life. He would love nothing more than to adopt you into His family and reserve you a home in His eternal kingdom. God's will is to deliver the addict from the nightmare of his addiction. True peace and victorious living can be found in the "King of Kings, and Lord of Lords" (Revelation 19:16). The Bible clearly illustrates what we must do in order to be saved.

> That if you confess with your mouth Jesus as Lord, and believe in your heart that God raised Him from the dead, you will be saved; for with the heart a person believes, resulting in righteousness, and with the mouth he confesses, resulting in salvation (Romans 10:9-10).

If you have never done so, I would encourage you to call on the Lord Jesus Christ for salvation and deliverance. Don't delay, don't put it off! Invite Him into your life as your personal Lord and Savior.

As of the writing of this book, some forty-six years have transpired from the moment I received Christ as Lord and Savior. It has been over thirty years since God miraculously delivered me from bondage to alcoholism, drug addiction, gambling and sexual promiscuity. I no longer have to profess I am a recovering addict. I have fully recovered from the bondage that once haunted my daily living. Today, I am able to comprehend the words of Scripture when it proclaims, "he is a new creature; the old things passed away; behold, new things have come" (2 Corinthians 5:17). God's Addiction Recovery Plan is a program through which I believe God brought deliverance, recovery, peace, joy, and victory to my life. I believe God would have me share this victorious message with you. I long for you to experience the living reality of a God who loves you, who is concerned about you, and wants the best for you. The purpose of this book is to present Jesus Christ as the only true path of salvation, deliverance, victory, recovery and true freedom. My prayer is that God will use this book as an instrumental tool in leading others to His saving grace. I pray through this testimony God will instill within you the hope and promise of the risen Christ.

Chapter 2
Recognizing the Problem

Freedom Step One

I must acknowledge I am a sinner in need of deliverance from my sinful nature and behavior.

Romans 3:23
"For all have sinned and fall short of the glory of God."

1 John 1:8
"If we say that we have no sin, we are deceiving ourselves and the truth is not in us."

Romans 5:12
"Therefore, just as through one man sin entered into the world, and death through sin, and so death spread to all men, because all sinned."

Many will undoubtedly question, what does addiction recovery have to do with a sinner in need of deliverance? The first step of recovery from any problem is recognizing a problem exists. Addiction can certainly be compared to a destructive illness, and should be easily recognized as a problem. This is perhaps the single greatest obstacle to an addict's recovery. Admitting he has a problem is a rite of passage. The addict has a serious problem that affects everything and everyone he touches.

Pride is at the forefront of man's sinful nature and often prohibits him from recognizing he is the real problem. He believes he is strong, powerful, and capable of handling all the issues of life on his own, and boasts that he needs no one else. Man finds great difficulty in admitting or acknowledging he is wayward and guilty of sin. He demands his own way and has become a master of manipulation in his efforts to get what he wants. Nothing is beyond his capacity when he is determined to get what he feels is of necessity.

This attitude is quickly manifested in the example of children. The sinful nature of man does not take long to manifest itself. Man is born with an ingrained stubbornness, a propensity to have and demand his own way. One of the first evidences of sin is a child's insistence on having it his way. Children are born into this world as selfish creatures and often grow up to become selfish adults. How long does it take a child to cry for attention? What is the first thing a child does when he breaks forth from his mother's womb? He cries! From the time of his first breath, he demands attention and intends to get it. A child comes into the world desiring and demanding his needs, wants, and desires. He cries to be seen, heard, changed, fed, loved and pampered.

A child quickly learns how to conceal, deny, and lie about his disobedience. Children do not have to be taught how to lie, it comes quite naturally. To the contrary, a child must be taught to tell the truth. Likewise, they do not have to be taught to steal and cheat. All of these defective characteristics naturally flow and follow as a child begins to mature. Sin and undisciplined behavior are a result of the sinful nature inherited from Adam. Children must be taught to do what is right. The Biblical Path to Freedom teaches that man is born into this world with a propensity to do wrong. He is born in bondage to a corrupt and sinful nature. Children demonstrate a profound example of what God defines as the sinful nature. This age is not unfamiliar at all with children who commit crimes and unthinkable acts. Children are found guilty of raping, killing and even molesting one another. Billions of dollars are spent by retailers in their efforts to curtail and prosecute shoplifters, and many of them are children. More and more we are seeing children charged with adult crimes. Sin is a progressive spiritual disease eating away at its victims with a tenacious appetite bent on disobeying God.

Man has a problem defined by God as sin. Modern day philosophers, psychologists, psychiatrists, and sociologists find various means of justifying man's behavior. The world has mastered the art of covering up man's sinful tendencies. The baby is defined as a fetus to justify murder. The world refers to the homosexuals, transvestites and lesbians as those having an alternative lifestyle. We are told these lifestyles should be accepted as normal behavior, rather than viewing them as sinful according to God's standard. The world defines addiction as a disease and insinuates man is not responsible for his own behavior; therefore, society should not hold him accountable. The world is quick to place the blame on parents, schools, governments and environment. Take a good look around the planet. The world is sinking in an ever increasing and never-ending cesspool of evil. Man is visibly out of control. Terrorist and rouge nations are bent on promoting and carrying out their evil deeds. Sin is a progressive evil that will eventually destroy man if not contained. This is the primary reason we have laws that must be enforced, and the failure to do so only serves to create more wickedness. One of the great hindrances to an addict's recovery is the refusal of society to hold him accountable. Solomon gives us ample warning, "Because sentence against an evil work is not executed speedily, therefore the heart of the sons of men is fully set in them to do evil" (Ecclesiastes 8:11 KJV). Man does great harm to individuals and societies when he fails to hold people accountable. God will never be guilty of allowing man to escape the consequences of his sin.

The question then remains, why and how did the addict's problem begin? Where does the real root of this dilemma reside? At the root of the problem man can find and deal with the base reason for his captivity, bondage, or enslavement to drugs and alcohol. Addiction is the direct result of sin residing within. Sin can be defined as transgressing God's law or missing the mark of God's perfect righteousness. Man is born into a state of unrighteousness as an infant; it's not that man becomes unrighteous as he progresses in his existence. The Bible indicates man is born with a corrupt nature. He enters into this world in a defiled state which will be quick to manifest itself in sinful behavior throughout his life.

It's not only the addict who must deal with the sin issue. Sin manifests itself in many different ways through the lives of every human being. The sinner may prove to be a liar, an adulterer, a homosexual, a pedophile, a thief, a murderer, a sexual deviant, a drunkard, a drug addict or a gossiper. He may display a heart filled with greed, envy, jealousy, hatred, racism, lust, immorality, sensuality, and impurity. The Biblical Path to Freedom points to the reality that none are without sin and therefore all are separated from God. "There is none righteous, not even one" (Romans 3:10).

Sin can be found and is displayed in numerous aspects of man's rebellion. Those who perhaps may appear to be the essence of moral value and character are far from being sinless creatures. Regardless of what the sins of choice or detriment may be in a person's life, the root cause is a sinful nature in rebellion against God. Due to the sin nature, all men are born with certain weaknesses and character defects that propel them toward surrendering to sin, when their fault line is probed by temptation.

The truth finds all men equally sinful in the eyes of God. James writes, "For whoever keeps the whole law and yet stumbles in one point, he has become guilty of all" (James 2:10). There are no degrees or levels of righteousness, spiritual death, or physical death. God views all sinners as being in the same spiritual state. They are spiritually dead. Those caught in the darkness of spiritual death have no righteousness with regard to a relationship with God. Man's sin is the cause of spiritual and physical death. Regardless of the extent or number of sins, he is defined as spiritually dead in "trespasses and sin" (Ephesians 2:1). A great example of this can be illustrated with a dead body. A dead man is dead! Whether he was shot with one bullet or showered with many bullets, the man is physically deceased. There is no scale to define how dead he is, for there are no degrees of physical death.

The same example is true in a spiritual sense. It doesn't matter how many sins he has committed. He is not dead due to his particular sins; he is spiritually dead as a result of his sinful nature. He is born of this world with a nature bent toward sinfulness. For illustrative purposes, this could be defined as a spiritual disease of which all men must contend with. This is an area where addiction may be compared or illustrated as a disease, but it cannot be properly defined as so.

Leprosy in biblical days was quite common; it was also symbolic of sin, as the leper was deemed an outcast of society. They had their own communities and were forbidden to mingle with the public. They were considered unclean and cursed of God. Leprosy was a physical death sentence that only required time to manifest its destructive nature. The physical disease of leprosy serves as a great illustration as to the sinful nature of man.

All men are born with a sinful nature impacting their being in various ways and measures. Every human being has weaknesses, defects, and shortcomings which manifests themselves by sinful means. The drug addict and alcoholic have given their lives to substances of choice. Rather than bow to God in humble submission and fall under His management, the addict chooses to be controlled by a substance, rather than by the God who created him. The addict has yielded to something beyond his ability to control. He is enslaved by what he has given and yielded himself too. The same is true of the liar, adulterer, homosexual, child molester, thief and murderer. In the eyes of God, they are all equally spiritually dead and in need of a spiritual resurrection. Here is the promise and hope of the new life made available in Christ.

Like all men, addicts are infamous for insisting on doing things their own way, instead of God's way. He has given himself to a master of substance and Jesus said, "No one can serve two masters" (Matthew 6:24). The addict understands what it means to be mastered and owned. Addicts are in bondage to the substance they have given themselves too. The root of the problem is a refusal to put God first, and submit to His sovereign rule. The selfish nature of man drives him to insist on having things his way. The Creator believes in the principle of freewill and has given man the option as to what or who he will follow. Man can continue choosing his own way and drive himself into despair, or he can humbly submit to God's will, and allow Christ to be the One who sits upon the throne of his heart. When man allows God to sit upon the throne, rather than being the ruler of self, he will discover progress in moving forward on the Biblical Path to Freedom. God is then able to change the inner most part of the addict's nature and set him free from enslavement to sin. Man is going to be a slave to Christ, or he is going to be a slave to sin. If he is not enslaved to addiction, he will be enslaved by some other means of bondage. He is either bound by righteousness or unrighteousness. There is no neutral ground when it comes to the issue of sin. God has provided man with no other choices, he will choose to serve God, or he will choose to serve sin. Jesus spoke about the tragedy of men choosing darkness over light. "This is the judgment, that the Light has come into the world, and men loved the darkness rather than the Light, for their deeds were evil" (John 3:19).

God will accept nothing less than first place in a man's life. To place anything before God is to commit the sin of idolatry. Because He is man's Creator, God has the right to demand absolute allegiance, praise, adoration, and worship. When Jesus Christ died on the cross and arose from the dead, He won the right to demand that "every knee will bow, of those who are in heaven and on earth and under the earth, and that every tongue will confess that Jesus Christ is Lord" (Philippians 2:1011). When man refuses to submit himself to God, he submits to the sin that has overpowered him. As a result, he turns to other gods in an attempt to meet the desires of self. God made this demand of surrender not only to His chosen people, but to all of mankind when He said, "you shall have no other gods before Me" (Exodus 20:3). Man becomes a god unto himself when he determines to do things his own way, and the dark consequences of his choices are inevitable.

At some point and time in his life, the addict made a conscious choice to begin using drugs, alcohol, or become involved in some other type of addictive behavior. He yielded to the weaknesses probing his sinful and fleshly nature. The addict has continued forward in sin, and has given his life to whatever his sins of choice may be. Whether it be sex, drugs, booze, sports, entertainment, golf, fishing, etcetera; he finds himself consumed by it. It becomes a means and search to fill an empty spot within, a void punctuated by the absence of God. There is an emptiness found in the heart of a sinner. He is void of the spiritual life which was lost in the garden when Adam sinned against God. The drunkard and drug abuser, like all other sinners, seek to fill the void with their choice of sins that prey on their fleshly weaknesses.

Alcohol is just another drug, albeit a legal substance for adults. Addiction is not concerned as to whether something is legal or not; its only concern is with the destruction it brings to its victims. Prescription drug addiction and abuse run rampant throughout the United States. A piece of paper makes a drug no less addictive or destructive. When it is abused, it will become a problem that will eventually reap chaos, destruction, and havoc upon its victim. It will have the same devastating effect upon its victim, whether legal or illegal. God is not "one who shows partiality" (Acts 10:34), and nor is alcohol, drugs, addiction or sin.

No one becomes an addict overnight, and none are born as addicts except for an infant born to an addicted mother. Some may be born with a sinful weakness making them more susceptible to the ravages of addiction; but it's impossible for someone to be addicted to something they have never indulged in or experienced. A person may be allergic to a substance at birth, but he cannot be addicted. The abuse of drugs and alcohol is a sin affecting the spiritual, mental, emotional, and physical health of those who choose to participate. God's Addiction Recovery Plan, His word, and The Biblical Path to Freedom define drunkenness and drug abuse as sin. "Do you now know that the unrighteous will not inherit the kingdom of God? Do not be deceived---nor drunkards---will inherit the kingdom of God" (1 Corinthians 6:19). God would never condemn someone for having a mental or physical disease. Drunkenness is a result of abusing alcohol or drugs. To be high on drugs is to be intoxicated as someone inebriated with alcohol. It's simply a matter of the mind and body being adversely affected by a foreign substance.

Addiction only serves as a symptom to a much deeper problem, that of a sinful nature. The abuse of alcohol and drugs leads to addiction, and the actual root of the addict's problem has to do with a corrupt nature. Somewhere in the beginning of his addictive journey, the addict chose to indulge in whatever he is bound too. He chose to take his first drink, pop his first pill, run up his first fix, smoke his first rock, snort his first line, or watch that first pornographic movie. Sin resided in the addict long before he ever became addicted to whatever his sins of choice are. Perhaps due to some weakness caused by ingrained sin or a defective character, whatever the reason, somewhere along the road the addict was overcome by making a bad choice.

Conquering and overcoming any problem requires us to first recognize a problem exists. Recovery step one confronts the root of an addict's problem and recognizes the primary target of concern must be with the power of sin. The penalty for sin is death, spiritual and physical, both being the result of sin. Here is the problem an addict must honestly face and deal with to experience genuine freedom from his addiction. To truly break free from such bondage requires a personal encounter with Jesus Christ who came to "set the captives free" (Luke 4:18). Sin is defined as "transgressing of the law" (1 John 3:4).

Because of man's inherited sinful nature, he is born into a rebellious state of hostility against God. This rebellion leads some into the throws of alcohol and drug abuse. The result is dependency upon a substance which becomes a god to the person it owns or manages. What does the addict live for? Another drink, another fix, another high, or drunk, and in many instances, he will reach a place of willingness to do whatever is necessary to acquire his perceived need. He will rob his child's piggy bank, blow the monthly mortgage payment, allow his children or wife to go without, and steal from his own mother. His depravity has no bounds when it comes to satisfying the craving for more.

Addiction leads to other sins such as lying, stealing, adultery, and murder. The addict lives for another alcohol or drug induced stupor, yet the fix he longs for only contributes to drive him deeper into bondage. His problem is sin. The Biblical Path to Freedom demands a confession and acknowledgement of sin before the addict can progress toward finding the solution of spiritual life in Jesus Christ. This is the first step in God's Addiction Recovery Plan. Progress will never be made until he accepts the fact and origin of his problem. He must admit it, agree with God's diagnosis and take God's prescription if he is to experience true freedom from bondage. The remedy to his problem is found in a spiritual resurrection from the death holding him captive to a dark sinful nature. Only Jesus Christ can resurrect the dead, whether physically or spiritually. He alone is defined as "the resurrection and the life" (John 11:25).

The new life offered to sinners by Jesus Christ is the only means of experiencing a complete recovery from addiction. What good is a spiritually dead inactive addict? He is still an addict enslaved by sin. Here is the problem with recovery programs refusing to include Jesus Christ as the solution. Secular recovery programs do not share the truth in declaring man is sinful and in need of salvation; nor do they proclaim the message that Jesus Christ is the only means of deliverance. They miss the mark by neglecting the spiritual necessity of regeneration, and choose to opt for the principle of reformation. There is a refusal to teach that man can be free and become completely loosed from his addiction. Secular programs suggest man is free to choose the god of his own interests. They are not concerned about whether or not the addict serves and worships a false god. The philosophy and teachings of worldly recovery programs insist on carrying the burden of remaining an addict forever. This is because the addict's basic nature has not been changed. Secular programs know nothing of the spiritual transformation made available only in Jesus Christ. He is taught "once an addict, always an addict," and "once an alcoholic, always an alcoholic." His future will be burdened and stressed with the constant fear of falling back into active addiction. He is but a dry addict abstaining from his substance of choice. Even though he may not drink or indulge in drug use, he will remain in bondage to his addiction. According to this worldly philosophy and thinking, he will never rid himself of the problem.

Even though he chooses to abstain, he will be defined as an addict forever, and live the rest of his days in fear of returning to his addiction. Although some reform has been brought about by his abstinence, his underlying problem of a sinful heart remains. He is still an addict in the eye of his mentor, and will remain bound to the fears of his addiction. God's Addiction Recovery Plan declares if an addict is to truly overcome, he must admit to God his failure as a sinner, and ask Christ to save his life by eradicating his corrupt nature. He needs supernatural transformation and regeneration, rather than reformation which will never satisfy the need of his sinful heart.

Freedom step one is essential in leading the addict to faith in Christ and deliverance from addiction. The addict must come to agree with God instead of accepting the philosophies and religions of the world. Newness of life begins by placing oneself in agreement with the word and promises of God. A new perspective will open up when an addict agrees with the truth and begins a new journey of faith in Jesus Christ. This important step requires an act of faith. It exhorts the addict to agree with God and deal with the root cause of his addiction. Acknowledging and confessing sin is the addict's first step to deliverance and recovery on The Biblical Path to Freedom. God's Addiction Recovery Plan leads the addict to this fact: **I must acknowledge I am a sinner in need of deliverance from my sinful nature and behavior.**

Chapter 3

Tapping Into The Solution

Freedom Step Two

I must understand Jesus Christ paid the penalty for my sin and offers me a new life.

Romans 5:8
"But God demonstrates His own love toward us, in that while we were yet sinners, Christ died for us."

John 3:16
"For God so loved the world that He gave His only begotten Son, that whosoever believes in Him should not perish, but have eternal life."

2 Corinthians 5:21
"He made Him who knew no sin to be sin on our behalf, so that we might become the righteousness of God in Him."

Judicial systems around the world require a criminal to pay for his crimes against society. When his crime is of a serious nature, he becomes a threat and is deemed unworthy to live among those who choose to abide by the law. When a criminal is charged with a crime, tried, and found guilty, he is sentenced accordingly. It's the law! The law is implemented for the protection of those who will abide by it. When the law is enforced, it maintains civility and order in society. Imagine what a city or nation would experience if suddenly all law enforcement were removed. Chaos would almost immediately ensue, because men are particularly prone to evil when there are no restraints. Rules and laws are for the benefit of man and the society in which he dwells. When he dares to break the rules, there is a price to be paid in an attempt to protect society.

This same principle is true in a spiritual sense with regard to God's universal courtroom of justice. In the spiritual realm God is Judge, Juror and

Executioner. He has the final say in all matters and issues of spiritual justice. God created man and the world; therefore, He has the privilege of declaring and enforcing the rules. God has found man guilty of sinning against His law, and as a result He has imposed the sentence of death upon all.

The first man Adam violated the one law God had established in man's realm of responsibility. God implemented one prohibition upon man in the Garden of Eden.

> The Lord God commanded the man, saying, "From any tree of the garden you may eat freely; but from the tree of the knowledge of good and evil you shall not eat, for in the day that you eat from it you will surely die" (Genesis 2:16-17).

Think about it! What if life consisted of only one prohibition to contend with? Adam and Eve were permitted to go and do as they please, with one exception. The first two human beings were forbidden to eat of one tree in the garden and failed to follow this simple command. Their failure defined as sin was disobedience to God. They committed what was forbidden, and Satan has had a field day ever since. A crime was committed in the garden and it didn't take God very long to show up on the scene as Investigator, Judge, Juror and Executioner. Justice was to be meted out and the law had to be enforced. God could not overlook and wink at their sin. His law had been violated and had to be dealt with. God had forewarned Adam of the consequences should he violate the law of the garden.

What was Adam's initial response when God showed up on the scene? He ran and hid. This sounds strikingly similar to the behavior of an addict. Adam became paranoid and began to experience the emotion of fear. Addicts are well known for being paranoid; they have a habit of always looking in the rearview mirror, peeping out windows and expecting law enforcement to show up. Fear entered Adam's world as a result of his sin. Perhaps he was looking over his shoulder, wondering when the Enforcer would arrive; sure enough, the Lord came to town.

> They heard the sound of the Lord God walking in the garden in the cool of the day, and the man and his wife hid themselves from the presence of the Lord God among the

trees of the garden. Then the Lord God called to the man, and said to him, "Where are you?" He said, "I heard the sound of You in the garden, and I was afraid because I was naked; so I hid myself" (Genesis 3:8-10).

What was Adam so fearful about? Why was he so paranoid? He had violated the law of God and was now confronted with being accountable for his actions. He found himself running from the law, running from God, and his descendants have followed in his footsteps. Since the day that Adam violated the law of God, man has been born into the world as an outlaw in blatant rebellion, spending his days on the run. God had already executed the sentence of death when He arrived at the garden. Not only was the death sentence executed, a curse was placed upon man, the woman, the serpent and creation. Man lives in fear because deep within he is aware and understands judgment day is coming. "And inasmuch as it is appointed for men to die once and after this comes judgment" (Hebrews 9:27).

At the end of time, the Judge of all the earth will execute the final sentence of eternal life or eternal death. Those who die without an internal change to restore what was lost in the garden will face eternal death. They will be separated from God and all that is good forever. Those who have accepted Christ as the cure or antidote for their sin, will be changed, declared righteous, and be blessed with eternal life. God will pardon all who call upon Him for mercy and grace. There is an Old Testament story which aptly illustrates the deadly sting of sin and the cure available.

> The Lord sent fiery serpents among the people and they bit the people, so that many people of Israel died. So the people came to Moses and said, "We have sinned, because we have spoken against the Lord and you; intercede with the Lord, that He may remove the serpents from us." And Moses interceded for the people. Then the Lord said to Moses, "Make a fiery serpent, and set it on a standard; and it shall come about, that everyone who is bitten, when he looks at it, he will live." And Moses made a bronze serpent and set it on the standard; and it came about, that if a serpent bit any man, when he looked to the bronze serpent, he lived (Numbers 21:6-9).

These rebels had been judged for their rebellion and God was pouring out His wrath upon their sin. The bronze serpent they were to look upon for deliverance from the deadly snake bites was symbolic of the Christ to come. They would look upon the cross by faith in their promised Messiah or Savior. Man is in a spiritual state of death, infected with spiritual venom, and his only hope is Christ.

One of the most venomous snakes in the world is the Black Mamba Cobra. In most cases its toxic poison is a lethal death sentence to its victim, unless an antidote is received within a short period of time. Its bite is almost certain death for those unable to find help quickly. With regard to man's spiritual condition, the serpent in the Garden of Eden induced a lethal dose of spiritual venom when man accepted the bait and believed the lie. It immediately induced spiritual death that eventually led to physical death, "For as in Adam, all die" (1 Corinthians 15:22). As we saw in chapter two, the sentence God chose to impose upon all men was spiritual and physical death. Justice demanded a penalty for man's criminal offense against God. Should a man die in his sinful state, the final sentence of eternal death, also referred to as "the second death" (Revelation 20:14), will be executed with no chance of parole or a shortened sentence.

Man decides his eternal fate in this life which is sealed the moment he transitions into the next realm. He is confronted with two options during his earthly journey: eternal life in heaven, or eternal death in darkness. The deadly spiritual venom that has destroyed man's spiritual condition can only be reversed by God's prescribed antidote. Jesus Christ is God's only prescribed remedy for reversing the effects of the deadly spiritual venom that has produced man's spiritual dilemma. Whether the addict understands it or not, he is on the run from God, attempting to drown the pain of his guilt and fears with alcohol or drugs. He fails to understand that he cannot outrun God, and subconsciously is aware that a day of judgment will eventually find him. His sin will eventually catch up with him.

The Creator of man describes himself as a God of love, "for God is love" (1 John 4:8). God loves man so much that He decided to take man's eternal judgment upon Himself on the cross. In doing so, He offers salvation and deliverance to all who will turn to Him by faith. God the Father chose to make Himself known to man by sending His Son Jesus Christ into the world. His word tells us that Jesus came to earth as God in the flesh. "And the Word became flesh, and dwelt among us, and we saw His glory, glory as of the only begotten from the Father, full of grace and truth" (John 1:14). Jesus was God who existed in heaven for all eternity before coming to earth as a babe clothed in human flesh. He can rightly be called the God-Man; He had no beginning, nor does He have an end. In the Book of Revelation, Jesus Christ is defined as "the first and the last," (Revelation 1:17), "the beginning and the end" (Revelation 21:6). Paul gives us a good perspective on Jesus Christ in writing, "He is before all things, and in Him all things hold together" (Colossians1:17). God loved His prize creation so much that He actually came from heaven to pay the death penalty on man's behalf.

Jesus paid the penalty for our sin in full on the cross when He was crucified. Because He was the perfect Son of God, death had no power over Him. The grave could not hold Him, and the result was resurrection from the dead. This was to provide man a way of escape from the venomous poison that deems him as a sinner. "But God demonstrates His own love toward us, in that while we were yet sinners Christ died for us" (Romans 5:8). In a spiritual sense, man was bitten by a deadly venomous snake in the Garden of Eden. In Christ, an antidote was made available to save man from death.

God has offered salvation to all who will receive His Son and accept the sacrifice He made on man's behalf. Unless a man receives Christ, the remedy of His work will be of no effect to the sinner. Man must either pay an eternal penalty for his own sin, or someone must pay it for him. Jesus Christ took the penalty upon Himself; no one else could pay it because no other perfect man has ever existed. Because He was perfect and had no cause to be executed for sin, He was qualified to pay the penalty for others. Man has the responsibility of accepting the offer, if it's to be applied to his account. The redemptive, atoning work of Jesus Christ on the cross, offers a pardon to all who will simply believe and accept by faith His accomplishment. This is God's gift of salvation to man. As Jesus breathed his last breath on the cross, He made the great proclamation, "it is finished" (John 19:30). What was finished? Jesus came to earth with the express purpose of paying the penalty of man's sin, to make God known to man, and to extend His gracious hand of mercy. In doing so, He made salvation from sin and its condemnation available to all who would accept His grace. Forgiveness of sin is available only in Christ, and redemption is what the addict so desperately needs.

Only those who believe, adhere to, and accept the fact that Jesus paid the ultimate penalty for man's sin, can receive the pardon and newness of life available in Him. The religions of the world seek to reform man and make him presentable or acceptable to God. Religion promises to make man good enough to find God's favor and forgiveness through good works or deeds. Man cannot do enough good to gain favor and earn salvation or freedom from spiritual bondage. Good works and deeds are not sufficient in delivering man from the spiritually venomous poison that entered his being at the very moment Adam disobeyed God. Only Christ can restore unto man that which is lost and dead in sin; for only God has the power to raise the dead.

Through God's grace and infinite mercy, Jesus Christ offers a spiritual resurrection from the dead. He offers us a newness of spiritual life that will one day be followed by a physical resurrection from the dead. In God's Addiction Recovery Plan, man can do nothing to save and deliver self. He must throw himself completely upon the mercy and grace of God found in Jesus Christ. Man's means of salvation and freedom from the curse of sin must be reliant totally upon the completed, redemptive work of Christ on the cross. This is accomplished by simple repentance and faith. Jesus died and arose from the dead, and thereby offers us the same transition. In order to accomplish this great victory over death, He gave His own life. Jesus offers not only a fresh start, but an entirely new life, which can be received only in accepting Him by faith.

Jesus can speak calm to the storm raging within an addict's soul. Most of his storms are self-induced. The addict more often than not stirs up storms and leaves a path of destruction everywhere. There is nothing more marvelous than hearing Jesus speak the words, "hush be still" (Mark4:39) to a raging storm embedded in the human heart.

And there arose a fierce gale of wind, and the waves were breaking over the boat so much that the boat was already filling up. Jesus Himself was in the stern, asleep on the cushion; and they woke Him and said to Him, "Teacher, do You not care that we are perishing?" And He got up and rebuked the wind and said to the sea, "Hush, be still." And the wind died down and it became perfectly calm. And He said to them, "Why are you afraid? Do you still have no faith" (Mark 4:37-40).

God has spoken to the hearts of many addicts and continues to do so. He has calmed the storms of chaos in thousands once bound by addiction, and many who seemed beyond repair have been restored. Addicts once ravaged and devastated by the disastrous consequences of addiction have experienced restoration and hope. God is a Master at putting broken hearts and lives back together. The Lord desires to calm your storm and set you free. He can only do so when you submit to His means and methods. Man must come to God on His terms.

The addict needs help and his hope is in acquiring a new Master. He needs God to remedy an issue he is utterly incapable of resolving himself. The addicted have given themselves over to alcohol, drugs, or something else. It now becomes imperative for them to change their mind, make a firm decision, and give up the old life. The time has arrived for the addict to forsake his sin, turn from his own way, and turn to the Master who is able to meet the deepest need and desire of his heart. He needs to meet the Master of the wind, and come to know the One who is able to walk on the stormy waves and seas of life. The addict is desperately searching for peace in the midst of a great storm, seeking after joy, serenity, freedom, righteousness, peace and life. Freedom step two helps us to realize who we are, what we have done, and provides us with the remedy of our primary problem called sin. God is always standing at the door offering deliverance and salvation to those who will sincerely call upon Him. He is at the helm of life's stormy sea, waiting to speak calm to the raging storms. Is the Master perhaps knocking at your door today? "Behold, I stand at the door and knock; if anyone hears My voice and opens the door, I will come in to him and will dine with him, and he with Me" (Revelation 3:20).

God speaks to the heart of man through His word, convicting men of sin with the Holy Spirit. He speaks to the addict and bids him come. "Come unto Me, all who are weary and heavy-laden, and I will give you rest" (Matthew 11:28). The addict is familiar with the burden of his sin, although he may not understand it. Rest seems to evade him at every turn. Are you tired and weary? Do you need rest from the burden of your addiction? You'll never discover it by choosing to remain bound. You must turn to the only One who can remove the burden and give you rest from a weary soul. It's a choice!

Sin creates a tremendous weight upon the heart of a sinner. Forgiveness of sin is the great need of every human heart and is the only means of escaping the fear of judgment. The addict has burdened himself with a multitude of sins throughout his days of addiction. Day after day the burden of guilt tends to increase. Should the addict not receive relief, he will eventually break under the heavy load of guilt. God longs to forgive the addict, despite all he has done. All of man's sin is ultimately against the God who created him. Only God can provide the needed forgiveness that calms the raging storm and relieves the burden of guilt. The addict suffers much due to his own making. Throughout his life he has committed countless sins. He stands condemned and deserves nothing less than judgment, but good news is found in Christ. It doesn't matter what, how many, or how severe your sins may be; God extends His offer of forgiveness.

A good illustration is found in the biblical account of a woman who was caught in the act of adultery. The penalty for adultery was death by stoning. This woman was brought to Jesus by those who were quick to condemn her. Under the law she was guilty and had to pay the penalty for her crime. As she stood before Jesus, He demonstrated mercy and compassion. Rather than condemn her, He offered love and compassion as none other would do. And Jesus said, "I do not condemn you either. Go. From now on sin no more" (John 8:11). Perhaps this woman hung her head in guilt and shame, as she stood before His perfection and absolute purity?

Likewise, an addict understands this type of guilt, shame, and pain. It is a consequence of the various sins he has committed throughout his life. He often feels beyond the possibility of God's forgiveness, and perhaps thinks it is no longer available. An addict has done nothing beyond God's willingness and ability to forgive; he is never beyond divine redemption and deliverance. "If we confess our sins, He is faithful and righteous to forgive us our sins and to cleanse us from all unrighteousness" (1 John 1:9). The addict needs to ask and it will be granted, for God will never act contrary to His proclamations. He longs to extend forgiveness of sin and forever cleanse us of it. Will you call on God to request His forgiveness and cleansing from sin? If so, your life promises to never be the same.

God calls on each of us to make decisions as to our eternal destiny. Making matters right with God enhances our ability to rectify issues with ourselves and others. Man must choose to either continue in his quest of sin, or turn his life over to the management of Christ. If you have never accepted Jesus Christ as your personal Lord and Savior, perhaps today is the day? It's time to consider taking a step of faith towards progress in God's Addiction Recovery Plan. The Biblical Path To Freedom leads the addict to this fact: **I must understand Jesus Christ paid the penalty for my sin and offers me a new life.**

Chapter 4
Making The Decision

Freedom Step Three

I must understand salvation is a free gift and requires a heart decision on my part.

Romans 6:23
"For the wages of sin is death, but the free gift of God is eternal life in Christ Jesus our Lord."

Ephesians 2:8-9
"For by grace you have been saved through faith; and that not of yourselves, it is the gift of God; not as a result of works, so that no one may boast."

Revelation 3:20
"Behold, I stand at the door and knock; if any one hears My voice and opens the door, I will come in to him and will dine with him, and he with me."

We have learned and established this biblical fact: "the wages of sin is death" (Romans 6:23). Having such knowledge brings man to a place of decision. He must choose to remain in his state of spiritual death, or accept the spiritual life offered to him in Jesus Christ. When man is confronted with truth, he finds himself at a crossroads of decision and must choose to accept or reject what he has learned. His decision will determine his future direction and destiny. God's precious gift to man is eternal life; a new life that begins with true biblical faith in Christ. A genuine decision for Christ goes far beyond the bounds of religion. Accepting the gospel and acting upon it brings man into a personal relationship with the God of creation.

Jesus Christ claimed to be "the way, and the truth, and the life" (John14:6). As life Himself, Jesus Christ alone can impart spiritual life to others. He is the One who created, sustains, and maintains all things. Through Jesus Christ, God offers the addict a new life. Eternal life begins with God's gracious promise of forgiveness and provides man with a quality state of living in his current existence. God has no desire for anyone to continue living a miserable existence in spiritual death, separated from His love and all that is truly good. He wants us to have His best and experience life to the fullest. Man can discover and experience the purpose of God for his life.

God created man to be filled with peace, joy, happiness, righteousness and purpose. Those who reject Him will never experience the reality of His existence. They are incapable of enjoying life because they have no spiritual unction, knowledge, wisdom or understanding. There is no spiritual life for those without Christ. They have a physical body that eats, breathes, and sleeps; but they are completely dead to the things of God. They have been separated from the life of God by sin. Eternal life begins with resurrection from the spiritual death man suffered as a result of Adam's sin in the Garden of Eden. This is where spiritual and physical death began. The scourge of death has been passed down to all men from their first ancestor. Man is confronted with a choice of eternal life or eternal death. He must opt to continue in spiritual death or receive the newness of life offered by Jesus Christ. God has blessed man with the free will to choose; he chooses his eternal destiny by determining to continue going his own way, or opting to accept God's way. God's way is Jesus Christ, the only means of experiencing truth. He offers men a new life, a new start, a new lease. Man must be willing to turn from his old lifestyle, make a conscious decision to turn from sin, and call on the Lord for salvation. David in his hour of distress called out to God. "The cords of death encompassed me, and the terrors of Sheol came upon me; I found distress and sorrow. Then I called upon the Lord: O Lord, I beseech you, save my life" (Psalm 116:3-4). Although David was not an addict, he was familiar with distress and sorrow. The addict is no stranger to these emotions and must come to understand that he sits at the doorstep of God's mercy and grace. Only God can deliver or save man from the sin, distress, and sorrow he experiences.

It cannot be stressed enough that salvation is defined as freedom from the bondage and penalty of sin under the law. Salvation is the forgiveness, restoration, and impartation of eternal life as a free gift from God. When one thinks of a person being saved, he thinks of deliverance from some life-threatening danger. A man is standing on a rock in the middle of a river that is rapidly rising, and he is unable to swim. He waits in horror as the water rises toward his feet and suddenly sweeps him into the raging rapids; he is helpless and unable to save himself. Suddenly, a bystander follows the river bank beside the drowning victim, and eventually jumps in to rescue the man. This is a true story about a young man who was saved by someone else. He would have undoubtedly drowned, except for the man who saved his life. This is the state in which all men as sinners find themselves. They are drowning in a sea of sin and unable to save themselves.

The addict's life is at stake. He has no idea when the overdose may strike or when his heart may decide to cease its beating. He is susceptible to breathing his last breath at any moment due to his destructive behavior. In an hour of despair, he may choose to take his own life as the next barrage of stinky thinking bombards his mind. The next pity party may strike at any moment, bringing utter despair knocking at the door. The addict stands in need of deliverance and salvation. Because of the nature of addiction and the poor behavior it entails, the addict is subject to cross over into eternity with each passing day. What the addict fears most, may be the next issue he faces. "It is appointed for men to die once and after this comes judgment" (Hebrews 9:27).

The addict needs to take a good look in the mirror, consider who he is, and think about what he is doing. He needs to consider his end and understand the path he is traveling will eventually lead to his demise and death. All addicts eventually arrive at the same destination. It's simply a matter of when and how fast they reach the end of the road. Hospitals, mental wards, graveyards and prisons are filled with addicts who overran the cliff. Addiction threatens his physical life as each new day arrives.

God is continually standing at the door of the addict's heart seeking entrance. He stands with the gift of life and deliverance. A gift can only be classified as a gift. It cannot be earned, merited, paid for, or worked for in any capacity. Man could perform good works for an entire lifetime and never merit or gain the eternal life God offers as a gift. He could donate every dime he makes for his entire life to good causes and never merit salvation. God freely offers to man what he does not deserve; He longs to extend His grace, mercy, and forgiveness. The addict is on solid biblical ground when he feels unworthy, unclean, poor, wretched and filthy. "Blessed are the poor in spirit, for theirs is the kingdom of heaven" (Matthew 5:3). Man needs to recognize his spiritual poverty and cry out to God for help. Man, in his sin is poor, lost, wretched, useless, and condemned. It is utterly impossible for him to acquire a good standing with God based on religious practice or good moral works. Paul in his letter to the Ephesians made it abundantly clear when he wrote: "For by grace you have been saved through faith; and that not of yourselves, it is the gift of God; not as a result of work, that no one should boast" (Ephesians 2:8-9).

God is clearly a promoter of equal opportunity and equal spiritual status for all. Everyone is born into this world in an equal state of sinfulness. God's word emphatically declares, "There is none righteous not even one" (Romans 3:10). All men are saved or lost in the mind of God. Equally lost if we remain in our sinful state, and equally saved if we turn to Him by faith. In his letter to the Romans, Paul wrote, "For there is no partiality with God" (Romans 2:11). The world is guilty of partiality, is often considered unfair, and rightfully so. God's word gives man fair warning about judging men by their appearance and status in life. When it comes to the issue of salvation, God is not concerned about who you are, or what your worldly status is. God is more concerned about your eternal soul and where you will spend eternity. Heaven will be filled with people from all walks of life; likewise, suffering will plague those who refuse and reject the only means of salvation and deliverance available.

Step three on The Biblical Path to Freedom speaks of making a sincere heart decision to accept Jesus Christ as Lord and Savior. The spirit or the heart of man is the central part of his being that makes him tick. This is the entity of man that will exist somewhere forever as an everlasting soul. The great prophet Jeremiah said, "The heart is more deceitful than all else and is desperately sick; who can understand it" (Jeremiah 17:9). Oh, how true is this of the addict who is deceitful, desperately sick, and unable to be understood by others. What is the answer to Jeremiah's question? Only God can know the human heart and understand it. Jeremiah speaks of sin residing within and corrupting this central core of a man's person. The heart runs much deeper than the mere intellectual capacity of man's senses. Man needs to accept the written word of God as infallible and inerrant truth, rather than accept the philosophies, ideas and thoughts of the world which are bankrupt and clueless when it comes to the issue of a man's heart.

Man must dig deeper than the intellectual part of his being in order to receive God's free gift of salvation. The intellectual capacity of man may certainly serve as an entrance way into his heart, but it cannot save him. Man needs to understand what he is doing when turning to Christ and there is nothing intellectually complicated about it. Religion makes salvation difficult and complicated; Christ makes it easily understandable. Man needs to turn to God with all of his heart, mind, and soul, if he is to truly receive the free gift of salvation and experience genuine deliverance. Jesus speaks of the simplicity of a child in illustrating genuine faith. This type of faith is needed when a man determines to turn to Christ.

> And He called a child to Himself and set him before them, and said, "Truly I say to you, unless you are converted and become like little children, you will not enter the kingdom of heaven. Whoever then humbles himself as this child, he is the greatest in the kingdom of heaven" (Matthew 18:2-4).

A child looks to his parents for safety, protection, provision and security. The child is incapable of caring for itself. Children trust and rely upon their parents without question, with a simplistic faith to meet their daily needs. Childlike faith issues from the heart, rather than with an intellectual capacity. They look to their parents with a simple belief that comes from the heart rather than the mind. Children seem to instinctively believe their parents will look out for their best interests. Because of their simplicity, children are much easier to lead in a decision for Christ than the adult whose mind has become clouded with the world's way of thinking. Jesus exhorts grown men to become as little children when they look to Him by faith. Unless a child is abandoned, forsaken, or abused, he will display a simple reliance upon his parents. He will display a trust that comes from the depths of his heart, soul, and mind. God speaks to us again through His prophet Jeremiah. "Then you will call upon Me and come and pray to Me, and I will listen to you. You will seek Me and find Me when you search for Me with all your heart" (Jeremiah 29:13).

There are few things that will move a parent more than the sincere heart wrenching desires of their children. Communication from one heart to another is a powerful force and motivator. God calls on men to focus on Him with their hearts, and cry out to Him from the very depths of their being. As a child in danger crying out with complete trust and earnest to a parent for salvation and deliverance, so we must do with God. Man reaches out to God with his heart, rather than his intellectual capacities.

Addicts have a profound propensity towards the stinky thinking acquired from the ways of the world. This twisted thinking proceeds from the heart. Man's mind in his sinful state is corrupted by thoughts developed by the world, religion, and self. His mind is profoundly affected by the condition of his heart. His entire being is impacted by the way he thinks. God's desire is that we focus our thoughts completely on Him and seek to have the heart changed by His redeeming power. Jesus enlightened us as to the hearts dark condition. He demonstrates the precept given in the wise words of Solomon who wrote, "For as he thinks within himself, so he is" (Proverbs 23:7). To think within oneself is to think with the heart. Jesus said,

> But the things that proceed out of the mouth come from the heart, and those defile the man. For out of the heart come evil thoughts, murders, adulteries, fornications, thefts, false witness, and slanders. These are the things which defile the man. (Matthew 15:18-20).

As long as the heart of man remains in a wicked state, it will produce wicked, dark, stinky thinking. The world is in a chaotic state due to man's way of thinking. He simply cannot help or save himself from it, because his mind has been bathed and saturated in it. God wants to transform our thoughts by giving us "the mind of Christ" (1 Corinthians 2:16). God is not interested in reforming man; He specializes in transformation, not reformation. The only hope for a wicked heart is a transplant performed by the Great Physician. The attempted reformation of man's heart is a futile effort and will never be sufficient to tame its wicked tendencies. Transformation is an issue of the heart, and requires a sincere decision on our part if it's to be experienced. Secular programs promise to reform those who will follow after their man-made philosophies and teachings. God promises to transform those who make a sincere decision that comes from the heart. He is searching for those who will dare to turn from the world's thinking and turn toward Jesus Christ by simple faith.

To seek God with all of our heart simply means to look to Him, call on Him, and focus on Him with all of our being. Jesus defined such faith as being the greatest of all commandments. "And you shall love the Lord your God with all your heart, and with all you soul, mind, and with all your strength" (Mark 12:30). Here is the essence of heart changing faith. Such belief comes from deep down, not merely through the intellectual capacity. Such seeking provokes us to believe Him with every fiber of our being. This is faith that produces a deep heart determination and commitment to follow Him all the days of our lives. It's the commitment of a lifetime, not for a few fleeting days, months, or years. Being bound to righteousness is the only addiction acceptable to God. It is the only course capable of freeing an addict from all other bondages. This is where real change and transformation forms within and creates the new man. Freedom step three brings us to a place of decision. God pleads with us to receive His free gift of salvation from the penalty of sin and be delivered from the curse of the law.

What does it mean to make-a-decision for Christ? It's of utmost importance to understand a decision for Christ is the determination to surrender to God without reservation. Once this decision is made, you have given up self, and turned complete control over to God. You are to become His slave, servant and child. God loves and therefore never abuses His children. He never beats His servants and is always righteous in dealing with His people. To be a slave of Christ is the utmost essence of life.

God's children are indebted to Him and called to a life of complete submission to His will. Man can never repay the debt he owes to God, and He doesn't expect us to attempt repayment. The redeemed can choose to display his gratefulness by faithful obedience and submission. A decision for Christ entails making a conscious decision of submitting and bowing to Jesus Christ as Lord and Savior. You must be willing to set aside your own ambitions, dreams, desires and yearnings in exchange for whatever God has in store. God never informs us first as to what He would have us do regarding His specific will and purpose. He insists that we come to Him on His terms with an attitude and willingness to do whatever He commands. The apostle Paul sums it up with a very adequate description by informing the child of God, "You are not your own. For you have been bought with a price: therefore, glorify God in your body" (1 Corinthians 6:19-20).

Jesus made it clear as to what type of commitment was required in coming to Him. He said to them all, "If anyone wishes to come after Me, he must deny himself, and take up his cross daily and follow Me" (Luke 9:23). This is not some mere intellectual consent to the deity of the Lord Jesus Christ. God requires a complete surrender of our lives to Him at the moment of decision. This is where real spiritual transformation and genuine change takes place in our lives, and nothing less is acceptable to God. He demands a complete surrender of self will, a signing over of all rights to Him. When a person reaches this place in life, real change is at the doorstep and God will swing the door of the kingdom wide open. Such commitment and change will produce a desire to please God at all costs. Here is where addiction must flee and make room for the will of God. The result is freedom from self, the world and sin. It's freedom from being enslaved to Satan who is the master of all who live without Christ.

Men without God are slaves to a cruel demonic master named Satan. Consider the life of a captive prostitute beholden to a pimp who essentially owns her. She has no say, nor will of her own; she is abused, beaten, molested, denigrated and maligned by the demonic agent of her bondage. The same is true of the addict who is beholden to his addiction. Satan is behind the addiction binding and destroying the addict. He is a slave driver who seeks to destroy those he controls and maintains power over. To be an addict is to be owned and overpowered by sin. The lifestyle of an addict has proven itself a million times plus to be a difficult path. It's one of the many ways of transgression leading to death, destruction, woe, and misery. Satan is a despot who drives his slaves deeper and deeper into a life of despair. He leads them to polluted streams, defiled wells of drink, and feeds his servants from unsanitary cesspools. He nourishes them at the hog troughs of the world, beats them into submission, and drives them through the desires of their carnal nature. He preys on the wicked heart, and with his lies promises man something he cannot offer or deliver. Through his many false promises, he keeps man in sinful bondage and enslaved to his fleshly desires. Remaining in this state of bondage is a choice the addict chooses in his continued rebellion against God.

God has provided a way out of Satan's dark domain, and the man who refuses God's prescribe method of escape is without excuse. We have the option of choosing to make a change of management, or remain in bondage to "the god of this world" (2 Corinthians 4:4). Satan will continue to manage a man's life as long as he chooses to remain in his sin. A change of management means a change of ownership. It's a decision to change the way our life is conducted, the means by which it's managed, and entails a total new way of doing things. The addict can choose to remain under the management of Satan and continue in his sinful state of spiritual death, or he can make a change of management with one right decision. When a person makes the choice of receiving Christ as his new manager, he will reject the old ways and turn aside from old management. It's a heart made decision; a choice to become a child of God, a servant and slave of Christ, rather than remain a slave of Satan and sin.

Freedom step three leads us to a place of decision. What we do is an eternal choice which we will live to regret or cherish. How often has the addict lived to regret a choice he made yesterday or today? He has spent a lifetime making bad decisions. The choices we make have great impact upon the consequences we will face tomorrow. All men make the choice as to whether they will turn their lives over to the Creator, or remain in their sin and serve unrighteousness? A decision for Jesus Christ is the only genuine solution to the addict's problem. If the addict is to truly break free from the sin that enslaves him, he must choose to make-a-decision for Jesus Christ as his Lord and Savior. There is no other true means of escaping the tormenting nightmare of addiction. Will you choose to remain an addict enslaved for eternity, or choose to serve a loving God who has your best interests at heart? God's Addiction Recover Plan and The Biblical Path to Freedom lead an addict to this fact: **I must understand salvation is a free gift and requires a heart decision on my part.**

Chapter 5

Acquiring The Promise

Freedom Step Four

I must repent and receive Jesus Christ as my personal Lord and Savior by faith.

Acts 3:19
"Therefore, repent and return, so that your sins may be wiped away, in order that times of refreshing may come from the presence of the Lord."

2 Peter 3:9
"The Lord is not slow about His promise, as some count slowness, but is patient toward you, not wishing for any to perish but for all to come to repentance."

Romans 10:9
"If you confess with your mouth Jesus as Lord, and believe in your heart that God raised Him from the dead, you shall be saved."

Here is a most critical step if the addict is to be successful on his journey toward recovery. God's Addiction Recovery Plan and The Biblical Path to Freedom hinge on the addict's decision for Jesus Christ through repentance and faith. As a sinner, the addict is traveling an unpleasant road that will ultimately lead to total destruction when followed to its ultimate end. The addict is like a tornado leaving behind a path of havoc, chaos, and destruction everywhere it makes landfall. The debris of destroyed relationships, marriages, families, finances, health and careers are strewn along its route. The addict never dreamed or imagined the pain and suffering his sin would incur upon himself, as well as others who stood in his destructive path.

At the end of his journey awaits a dead-end street, the memory of a wasted life, and eventually death. Some addicts travel much further down the road of destruction than others; many have reached the end of the cliff, looked over, and turned around before making the final plunge. Unfortunately, far too many have plunged head-first into an unending eternal state of misery. Some have stopped at different points along the road, turned back, and survived the nightmare of addiction. Sadly, many keep running, tumbling, barreling ahead in misery, lost and bound forever. The addict must realize he is on a destructive path; he is on a road with the promise of more heartache to come. Unless he makes a conscious decision to turn around and head in the opposite direction, his nightmare will continue as he crosses into the point of no return.

This biblical fact is not only true of the addict, but applies to all who do not have a personal relationship with Jesus Christ. Recovering addicts are very familiar with what is known as the bottom. The bottom is having fallen as far as one can possibly fall and there is no direction to look but up. It's the lowest and loneliest place inhabited by man on this earth; an experience of complete despair where the addict is willing to accept the end of his addiction by any means necessary. The bottom generally makes or breaks the addict. He churns in the bottom of a barrel and is brought to the brink of making-a-decision to turn around or plunge into eternity lost. It's a point, a place, a time when the addict sees the ultimate end of himself. On the bottom he is confronted with a moment of decision and decides he can no longer continue in the same direction. This is a critical moment and time in the life of an addict; he has reached the ultimate brink of despair. He will consider various means and methods of escaping the mental anguish and despair that his soul is experiencing. Only the addict knows when he has reached his bottom, it will be the end of the road, one way or the other. I have witnessed many I thought had reached their bottom, only to discover they had some distance remaining to travel. When an addict truly reaches his bottom, he will make-a-decision; however, he does not have to reach bottom before making the decision to turn around. On the bottom he finds himself in the valley of decision. "Multitudes, multitudes in the valley of decision, for the day of the Lord is near in the valley of decision" (Joel 3:14).

The addict will eventually become "sick and tired of being sick and tired." He's had it with the nightmare; it must come to an end, for he can bear to suffer no more. He can no longer deal with the destruction his addiction has imposed upon him, and something has to give. A rubber band can be stretched but so far before it snaps. The addict who reaches his bottom is on the verge of snapping. He has lived in an agony on earth beyond the capacity of a normal person to understand. Only someone who has been there can understand and empathize with the addict who is living out a tormenting nightmare.

All addicts at one time or another have experienced a taste of death on earth. Those in the latter stages of addiction live in an emotional and mental state of constant torment. It's an inevitable experience for those who travel the ultimate road of self-destruction; Death will surely manifest itself eventually. The path of addiction has led the addict to untold heartache, misery, and pain. He can only be understood by someone who has been there and experienced this dark pit. This is why support groups are so important and sometimes vital to an addict's recovery. As he has faced varied emotions and thoughts in his addiction, he will face much the same in recovery as he travels back up the same road he has been down. The depth of an addict's dependency is commensurate with the depth of his emotional, mental, physical, and spiritual health. He has suffered the familiar promise of God as found in Paul's letter to the Galatians regarding the law of sowing and reaping, "Do not be deceived, God is not mocked: for whatsoever a man sows, this will he also reap" (Galatians 6:7). In his confrontation at the "valley of decision," the addict must come to understand, he has brought all of these problems upon himself. He must accept the fact that he is the problem and not everyone else. It's time to take a long look in the mirror. The time has come for pointing the finger back at self rather than at others. Until an addict reaches this place and accepts this fact, there will be no hope of recovery.

He has spent years placing the blame for his problems upon someone or something else. It's time to deal with self and take responsibility for his own actions. Responsibility and accountability are rarely strong points of the addict who has developed a habit of being irresponsible and unaccountable for self. He has spent years or even a lifetime dodging, evading, avoiding and side-stepping his responsibilities. The only means of avoiding complete and final disaster is to turn around. The only credible path leading to genuine recovery is in the complete opposite direction from which he has traveled for so long.

Repentance is realizing you have been traveling in the wrong direction and making a conscious decision to turn around. God's word gives us an excellent illustration of the road that all addicts travel. It's often referred to as the story of the Prodigal son (Luke 15:11-21). The Prodigal son reached his bottom wallowing in a pigpen of filth, abasement, and stench.

And He said, "A man had two sons." The younger of them said to his father, "Father, give me the share of the estate that falls to me." So he divided his wealth between them. And not many days later, the younger son gathered everything together and went on a journey into a distant country, and there he squandered his estate with loose living. Now when he had spent everything, a severe famine occurred in that country and he began to be impoverished. So he went and hired himself out to one of the citizens of that country, and he sent him into his fields to feed swine. And he would have gladly filled his stomach with the pods that the swine were eating, and no one was giving anything to him. But when he came to his senses, he said, "how many of my father's hired men have more than enough bread, but I am dying here with hunger! I will get up and go to my father, and will say to him, Father, I have sinned against heaven, and in your sight; I am no longer worthy to be called your son; make me as one of your hired men." So he got up and came to his father. But while he was still a long way off, his father saw him and felt compassion for him, and ran and embraced him and kissed him. And the son said to him, "Father, I have sinned against heaven and in your sight; I am no longer worthy to be called your son."

This is the story of a son who decides to leave his father's home in search of pleasure and self-fulfillment. The son had all he ever needed or wanted while he was in his father's home. He made-a-decision to rebel against the security of his home, and demanded his father give him an inheritance. He was soon on his way, chasing after worldly pleasure. The world was his to gain and he was determined to have it all. The neon lights of the night captivated him with such thoughts as "the world is yours." He left home with an inheritance in his pocket, and headed out for a life in the fast lane. When the money ran out, he found himself not only feeding pigs, but living with them as well. He had lived a riotous, rebellious, and sinful life, choosing to go his own way against the will of his father and loved ones. He thought he knew best and was determined to fulfill his own earthly dreams. Here is an ample illustration of all who determine to live in rebellion against God. The recovering, recovered, and practicing addict can relate to this story. This story of the Prodigal son aptly describes the life of addiction with preciseness as few others illustrate.

One day he discovered his financial inheritance was depleted and found himself at the bottom, in a pig sty, slopping hogs. At one time he had a promising future, a good family, plenty to eat, and a place of employment, but the good times were well behind him now. The good old days had long ago been left behind in his haste to search out after the world. He had destroyed them all with the choice to do his own thing and go his own selfish way. He now finds himself at the end of a miserable journey. He has hit bottom and begins to consider his own condition. Living and eating with pigs has brought him to a place where he is willing to consider his dilemma; he now sits at a dead-end street where he can look around and come to his senses. It is time take a good hard look at self, understand where he came from, where he's been, where he's at, and where he desires to go. This can prove to be a sobering moment for the addict.

As the light of truth breaks through to penetrate the darkness, he begins to understand how he arrived at his current status. Suddenly, he remembered where he had come from. He had left the comforts of a secure home many years ago. Looking back and reflecting he determines that perhaps it wasn't such a bad place after all. Maybe in his mind he traced his steps back from the very day he had left his father's house. Most likely he remembered all the fatal mistakes and decisions that brought him to his current misery. He understands his mistakes and errors in determining to go his own way, and begins to regret ever making the decision to do his own thing. The way he had been living was far beyond the desires and wishes of his father. The Prodigal son finds himself in "the valley of decision" (Joel 3:14). God's Addiction Recovery Plan and The Biblical Path to Freedom require an addict to make a decision. It's time for his final answer to the question, "what am I going to do with the rest of my life?" The proper decision is to turn around and head in the opposite direction.

Coming to his senses, the Prodigal son made the correct decision. He has made a decision that would deliver and save him from temporary and eternal destruction. His decision was to return home to his father and seek forgiveness. A new attitude and outlook on life has taken control. He is now willing to do whatever it takes, whatever is necessary to escape the reoccurring nightmare he has lived in for years. Here is where the addict will find victory and begin his journey toward complete recovery. Considering himself unworthy to be his own father's son, he determines to return and ask his father to make him a hired servant among his household. Upon making his decision, he got up, left the pig pen and headed home. His journey would lead to recovery, restoration, victory, righteousness, peace and joy. His transformation had begun, he became a new man in the "valley of decision" (Joel 3:14). He had followed a distant path of destruction, reached his bottom, and was now willing to do whatever was necessary to make and keep things right.

He is now confronted with making the long trip back home and must travel back up the same road he had previously traveled down. On his return journey he would once again face all the temptations, trials, and urges of fleshly pleasure he had once submitted and given himself too. At this point however, he had a greater understanding of these obstacles. They must be avoided, evaded, dodged, and denied, or he will find himself back in the pigpen. The road back would be the same distance as what he had already traveled. Getting back home would not be without temptation and struggle. Traveling downhill seems to be a rather smooth ride in the beginning, but cruising down the road of destruction is like a snowball rolling downhill. It's that wall at the bottom that stops the addict in his tracks. He now faces an uphill battle in his quest to get back home, and will be confronted with all of those pleasures that he faced and experienced on the way down. Temptation to turn back will be sobriety's primary enemy. The bait will be dangled at every turn, corner, junction, and crossroads. He must not stop and look back! The key is a fixation upon the destination for which he has determined. He must set his eyes steadfast on the journey at hand. He must make a firm resolve to set the old life behind him and press on with the new life awaiting.

The addict must not delay his decision to turn around and head back home. This can be a fatal mistake, and procrastination is no stranger to the addict. This critical juncture on The Biblical Path to Freedom must not be delayed, there must be no hesitation. Stinky thinking will suggest putting it off until tomorrow. This is one decision that cannot wait on a tomorrow that will never come for the procrastinator. The addict cannot hesitate to begin his return journey. He must begin immediately! Jesus found Himself in the company of two particular men and called them to follow Him. They both initially agreed, but followed up by placing themselves in a state of procrastination. Stinking thinking was allowed to creep in.

> And He said to another, "Follow Me." But he said, "Lord, permit me first to go and bury my father." But He said to him, "Allow the dead to bury their own dead; but as for you, go and proclaim everywhere the kingdom of God." Another also said, "I will follow You, Lord; but first permit me to say good-bye to those at home." But Jesus said to him, "No one, after putting his hand to the plow and looking back, is fit for the kingdom of God" (Luke 9:59-62).

Procrastination for the addict is always a recipe for disaster. These men refused to follow the commands of God and failed to follow Christ immediately. They chose to consider other pressing issues as being more important, insisting on putting matters off until another day, because their priorities were twisted and out of order. One man wanted to bury his father who was not yet deceased, and it could have been years before his father would actually die. The other wanted to return and say goodbye to his family. Chances are when he returned home to say good-bye, something else would arise, or he would be influenced by his family to stay at home rather than follow Christ. God's Addiction Recovery Plan and The Biblical Path to Freedom require action now, for tomorrow may be too late. It's time for the addict to set his priorities in order by placing salvation and deliverance at the top of his list. Nothing can be allowed to stand in the way! Putting it off until tomorrow may be the final mistake for the addict. Tomorrow can be a fatal and tragic error when it comes to a decision to repent and receive Christ. The addict may never see tomorrow; he may overdose today or tonight. He may breathe his last breath ten minutes from now by drowning in his own vomit, or in a bathtub. Paul emphasized the urgency of getting it done today when he said, "Behold, now is "the acceptable time, now is the day of salvation" (2 Corinthians 6:2). The addict who dares to put off salvation, deliverance and recovery until tomorrow is flirting with disaster. Today may be the last opportunity he has, for God may pull the plug and drop the curtain before tomorrow arrives.

The Prodigal son did not procrastinate in returning home. He must have left the pigpen with great eagerness and set his face steadfast toward the long journey back. Procrastination was not in the picture; the urgency of the moment required no delay. He would soon discover a marvelous truth, for when his father saw him coming, he ran to meet him with open arms. His father received him back into the household not as a hired servant, but as a full-fledged child with all the rights and privileges which had been forfeited in his previous departure. The son was met with his father's heart of compassion, mercy and grace. The son was undeserving and did not merit the way his father received him back into the home. He was forgiven, his losses were restored, and he received a new lease on life; the pigpen became a nightmare of the past. The addict can know that God will meet him with open arms on his road to recovery. Regardless of where you have been and what you have done, God stands waiting to receive you into His arms.

The Prodigal son aptly depicts the story and plight of an addict. The addicted has traveled a road of destruction and has sinned against God. Like all other sinners, the addict at some point in life decided to go his own way, rather than follow God's prescribed path. The Psalmist gives us some insight into the plight of those who persist in disobedience.

There were those who dwelt in darkness and in the shadow of death, prisoners in misery and chains, because they rebelled against the words of God and spurned the counsel of the Most High. Therefore, He humbled their heart with labor; they stumbled and there was none to help. Then they cried out to the Lord in their trouble; He saved them out of their distresses. He brought them out of darkness and the shadow of death, and broke their bands apart (Psalm 107:10-14).

The addict will find himself wallowing in a pigpen of squalor on earth; filled with despair, hunger, thirst, emptiness, loneliness, discontentment, and disappointment. Some descend more rapidly into the pit than others, but the pigpen is always waiting at the end of the road. Destruction has followed the addict to the end of his long adventure in sin; and long before the addict reaches the pigpen he begins to smell the stench. He will discover that his own clothes will reek of the dreaded odor. The pigpen is undoubtedly one of the most disgusting smells one can ever experience. Living in the pigpen is a way of life the addict knows all too well.

God knows and understands this road the addict has traveled. His perfect will and desire, is for none to travel this wretched path leading to destruction. The addict is only one of many who insist on going against God's will, demanding to have his own way. God set forth prohibitions for a reason. When God's principles, rules, laws and statutes are violated; inevitably, there will be unpleasant consequences. Most addicts insist on learning the hard way because they are stubborn, bull-headed, and intent on having it their way. Whether or not the addict has reached the end of his road, or is traveling on in this path of destruction, God's desire is for him to turn around. Just as the addict first chose to head down the road leading to destruction, he can make the decision to turn back at any time. He must make a turn from heading down the path of sin, forsake the path leading to his destruction, and turn toward The Biblical Path to Freedom. God is continually pleading with man to turn around, make things right and head home. This is biblical repentance, a conscious decision to turn around, reject sin, reject the ways of the world, and call out to God for salvation through faith in Jesus Christ. This is the only way and means of true freedom. It's a decision which will break the addict loose from the chains of sin that bind and enslave him.

As with all other sinners, addicts are following after the ways of the world. They are fixated on chasing after worldly things, worldly pleasures, fleshly desires and sinful temptations. The alternative is a conscious decision to turn around. Repentance is a conscious decision or determination to live God's prescribed way and forsake the world. The addict needs to make Jesus Christ the Master of his life and thus become obsessed with the truth. The individual who truly repents is presenting his life to Christ, asking God to take him and do with him as He pleases. To repent and make-a-decision of faith in Christ is to turn one's life completely over to the sovereign management of God. The addict must learn to pray as Jesus prayed in the Garden of Gethsemane, "Your will be done" (Matthew 26:42). The time for going one's own way must come to an end. Addiction ends with a decision to go God's way and follow His path.

With God's help and enablement from the day of decision forward, the addict must seek to do as God directs. Jesus Christ must become the recovering addict's number one priority on his recovery journey. He has become the property of God by setting aside self-will, and is now God's sole possession. As the Great Physician, God is well able to save, cleanse, heal, and deliver from sin. God's grace and mercy are extended when we accept ourselves as sinners in need of forgiveness, and understand that forgiveness can be found only in Jesus Christ. You must decide to surrender your life by giving God unconditional control; it's a decision that must come from the heart. God's word declares, "That if you confess with your mouth Jesus as Lord, and believe in your heart that God raised Him from the dead, you will be saved" (Romans 10:9). In the letter of Second Peter, we see that God "is not willing for any to perish but for all to come to repentance" (2 Peter 3:9). God's desire is for everyone to be saved, blessed, fulfilled and content in life. God's best for man is impossible unless he takes a step of faith, repents and turns to Christ.

The key to victory is seeing self as God sees us. As we have previously learned, God defines all men as wretched sinners. One of the godliest men in the Bible said of himself, "Wretched man that I am! Who will set me free from this body of death?" (Romans 7:34). The addict needs to see himself as a wretched sinner in need of God's mercy and grace.

This is often contrary to what psychiatrists and psychologists would have man to believe. Many of them would say man's problem is low self-esteem. They would claim he is basically good and only needs to discover the goodness of self. To the contrary, God says man is a wretched sinner and there is no goodness in him. "There is none righteous, not even one" (Romans 3:10). A man once referred to Jesus as "good Teacher" (Mark 10:17). Jesus replied, "Why do you call Me good? No one is good except God alone" (Mark 10:18). Man, in his sinful state possesses nothing good in the eyes of God; therefore, he must come to agree with God and cry out for the goodness of God to take up residence in his heart. God specializes in changing the vile and wretched into something beautiful and marvelous. As an ugly worm wraps itself up and eventually emerges as a beautiful butterfly, God desires to do the same for the wretched sinner via a spiritual metamorphosis. He alone has the power to bring about a miraculous work in the life of an addict. Thousands of former addicts can testify and bear witness that Jesus Christ saves and delivers from addiction.

Jesus referred to this miraculous transformation when He declared, "Truly, truly, I say to you, unless one is born again he cannot see the kingdom of God" (John 3:3). Repentance and acceptance of Jesus Christ as Lord and Savior must be completed before one can move forward on The Biblical Path to Freedom. When an individual accepts Jesus Christ as his personal Lord and Savior, he is immediately set free from the condemnation of sin (Romans 8:1), and is no longer subject to the penalty of the law. The addict will receive a new life, a new start, and enter into a personal relationship with God as his Heavenly Father. Perhaps it's time for you to accept a new lease on life? This new status consists of peace, love, joy, fulfillment, righteousness and eternal life. God has a plan and purpose for each of His creatures. There is no turning back to the old life once this step is embarked upon. The old man will be defined as dead and the new man will arise within those who have been born again. This new man must begin to see himself for what he is, "a new creature" (2 Corinthians 5:17), as defined by the word of God. He must put the past behind him and press forward in the new life God has blessed him with. He is on a new road that leads to a life of abundant living in Christ, and is now able to follow the instructions given by Paul: "Forgetting what lies behind and reaching forward to what lies ahead, I press on toward the goal for the prize of the upward call of God in Christ" (Philippians 3:13-14).

The new birth propels men toward becoming more like Christ. This is a new path, a new journey into an exciting adventure filled with God's presence and purpose. At this point you should have made the decision to accept Jesus Christ as your personal Lord and Savior. If you have not made this critical decision, please pray the following prayer with all your heart, mind, and soul.

Dear God in heaven, I come to you in the name of Jesus Christ. I confess I am a sinner and spiritually dead in sin. Lord, I need the forgiveness and deliverance that only you can provide. At this moment, I make-a-decision to repent, turn from my sin, turn from the world, and turn to Jesus Christ by faith. I acknowledge that Jesus Christ was God in the flesh; that He died on the cross for my sin, and arose from the dead. Lord, I confess with my mouth that you are the One and only true God. I ask you to forgive me of all my sin, wash me, and make me a new creature through the new birth. I agree to give up my own life and become all you would desire of me. Lord, I invite you into my life as my personal Lord and Savior from this moment forward. Lord, thank you for coming into my life. Take me and do with me as you will. I submit to your will, purpose, and plan for my life from this day forward. Please help me to persevere in my commitment and help me to overcome those areas in my life that are displeasing to you - Amen.

Forward progress in God's plan and purpose cannot be made until the new birth has been appropriated. Being born again (John 3:3) is an essential element of traveling The Biblical Path to Freedom. God's Addiction Recovery Plan leads the addict to this fact: **I must repent and receive Jesus Christ as my personal Lord and Savior by faith.**

Chapter 6

Accepting A New Status

Freedom Step Five

I must accept by faith the assurance of a new birth, and understand I am a new creature with a divine nature.

John 3:3
"Jesus answered and said to him. Truly, truly, I say to you, unless one is born again he cannot see the kingdom of God."

2 Corinthians 5:17
"Therefore, if any man is in Christ, he is a new creature; the old things passed away; behold, new things have come."

2 Peter 1:4
"For by these He has granted to us His precious and magnificent promises, so that by them you may become partakers of the divine nature, having escaped the corruption that is in the world by lust."

The moment an individual takes freedom step four, the Bible proclaims him to be a born-again follower of Christ. The Christian received new life when he said yes to Jesus Christ as his personal Lord and Savior. Paul defines the Christian as a new creation. "Therefore, if any man is in Christ, he is a new creature; the old things passed away; behold, new things have come." (2 Corinthians 5:17). A supernatural spiritual transformation has taken place in the inner most being of the person who has truly been born again. This supernatural transformation is performed by the Holy Spirit (God), who implants the very image and mind of Jesus Christ into a person's being. Although a follower of Christ resides in the same body, he is no longer the same person internally. The Holy Spirit has taken up residence in the Christian and will oversee the maturation process of the new man. This transformation will be immediate and progressive in nature. The born-again believer has been empowered and predestined to become what God has already predetermined.

These questions will inevitably arise: What does God have in store for me, and what is His will for my life? His desire is for us to become more like Jesus Christ. This will be performed by a process known as progressive sanctification. God has planted "the mind of Christ" (1 Corinthians 2:16) within your inner being. The new birth, the Holy Spirit's presence and the mind of Christ will necessitate spiritual growth, development, and maturity. God has actually planted a new nature within; whereas, "you may become partakers of the divine nature" (2 Peter 1:4). This divine nature will grow, develop and mature to bring about character changes and attitudes.

A physical new born infant must develop and mature. The same is true of the new person you have become through the new birth. The spiritual man begins a journey of growth from the standpoint of being a spiritual babe in Christ. He will begin to grow with the goal of becoming a spiritual adult. His ultimate destiny is to become more and more like Christ Himself in character.

The new man's rate of spiritual growth can be enhanced or stunted by poor habits, spiritual diet, thinking, choices, attitudes, and behavior. The Christian has been called to do as God instructs in humble obedience. If you are to grow and develop into the person God desires, you must quickly learn that obedience is of utmost importance. You have perhaps followed many paths that led you through one disastrous experience after another. Jesus points us to the correct path which must be followed in truly discovering and experiencing life the way it was intended.

> Enter through the narrow gate; for the gate is wide and the way is broad that leads to destruction, and there are many who enter through it. For the gate is small and the way is narrow that leads to life, and there are few who find it (Matthew 7:13-14).

Until a man is born again, he is traveling the broad way that leads to destruction. The practicing addict who hits bottom has found himself one step, one breath, one heartbeat away from eternal destruction. He is guilty of traveling a path of stubbornness, death, disobedience, defiance, waywardness, destruction, and rebellion. Hopefully you have made the decision to turn away from sin, and turn to Christ as Lord and Savior? If so, you have entered the way that leads to life. You are on the path that will direct you to a momentous victory. The narrow way Jesus spoke about is The Biblical Path to Freedom.

Your primary purpose and focus should be seeking, following, and obeying God as He leads you in this new journey and adventure. Along the path you will need to frequently stop and follow the exhortation of Jesus. "So I say to you, ask, and it will be given you; seek, and you will find; knock, and it will be opened to you" (Luke 11:9). God calls on His children to obey His every command and be diligent to "seek first His kingdom and His righteousness" (Matthew 6:33). This is The Biblical Path to Freedom that leads to the promise and experience of abundant life. In Christ, the recovering addict has found new life, new purpose, and a new direction. He has a new path and lease on life; he has already begun his journey toward recovery, and the slate has been washed clean. There is now a purpose, something new to live for, somewhere to go, and something important to accomplish. You have begun a new way of living which will eventually lead to all you have overlooked, missed, and neglected in the past.

Here you will find true meaning and purpose in life. God has a marvelous plan in store for you. God has promised to reward "those who seek Him" (Hebrews 11:6). Your future will be bright as you diligently follow God's Addiction Recovery Plan. I never dreamed or had any idea that one day I would be writing a book titled: God's Addiction Recovery Plan. Living for God is an exciting adventure and He has established a blueprint to be followed as we travel this journey. God's foundation is Jesus Christ and the written word of God, a manual that is sufficient for all the Christian needs to know. An entire new life lies ahead of the individual who looks to Christ by faith. It will be a journey of faith leading to an eternal home prepared in heaven. Jesus made this fact vividly clear to His disciples. "For I go to prepare a place for you; if I go and prepare a place for you, I will come again and receive you to Myself, that where I am, there you may be also" (John 14:2-3).

God has a marvelous and wonderful plan in store for our present and future interests that will erase the past. You're a child of God called to spiritual growth and godly behavior. God will require you to grow, mature, and begin to act as one of His children. Don't expect to grow up overnight; you have some catching up to do. By spending time in God's word, praying, and fellowshipping with other believers, you will learn to behave, look like, and walk like a child of God. As children often take on the attributes and characteristics of their earthly parents, the Christian will one day bear the image of his Master and Maker. "Just as we have borne the image of the earthly, we will also bear the image of the heavenly" (1 Corinthians 15:49).

God has blessed His people with the church to assist in developing this new-found way of life. He has given us the Bible to guide, instruct, reprove and correct. "All Scripture is inspired by God and profitable for teaching, for reproof, for correction, for training in righteousness (2 Timothy 3:16). God's written word will direct you down the proper path, lead you in recovery, and produce a fruitful life. He has given you the Holy Spirit who resides within your earthen vessel with the promise to never leave. God's Spirit will now lead, guide and direct you by the word of God and His sovereign power. God's word must always find first place in discerning His will, purpose, and plan. He will bring new people into your life to help you along the way and assist you in a diligent quest to become more like Christ. Becoming more like Christ is a daily process of which you will discover to be a lifelong quest of growth by feeding on spiritual milk and meat.

You will quickly discover and notice the existence of an unredeemed body. While the Bible defines the Christian as a new creature, the exterior portion of our humanity has not undergone any change. We have the same body that was with us prior to the new birth. The unredeemed body remains subject to sin, sickness, temptation, carnal desire, death and the consequences of sin. It's important for the Christian to strive and set aside those things which bring destruction to the physical body.

Those things would certainly include alcohol, unnecessary drugs and nicotine. Paul encourages the believer to act regarding the carnal flesh. "Therefore, I urge you, brethren, by the mercies of God, to present your bodies a living and holy sacrifice, acceptable to God, which is your spiritual service of worship" (Romans 12:1). Do not be discouraged; remember, God is in control and will bring you through it. Battles are inevitable! The spiritual storms will sometimes rage, as the spirit, God, and the unredeemed flesh battle it out. Victory will not always be pleasant and swift. A war between two fighting factions deep within will be evident at times. Keep in mind, if you're truly His and know it, Jesus Christ has already won the battle. Victory will come!

Paul advises the Christian that his body is "a temple of the Holy Spirit" (1 Corinthians 6:19). The Christian should strive to set aside those things which bring harm to his earthly temple. The believer has a great promise with regard to a future body. The Bible teaches that God's people will one day receive a new body, a glorified body custom fitted to inhabit the new kingdom to come (1 Corinthians 15:42). Until then, the Christian must learn to contend with and subdue his unredeemed vessel.

This is all part of the spiritual growth process of sanctification. You will discover your unredeemed body will inevitably demand forbidden and carnal desires. The best way to defeat ungodliness is to starve it. Looking at, listening to and reading the wrong things will produce fleshly desires. Spending time in the wrong places will prompt worldly thinking. Fleshly desires will at times seem irresistible and you may fall to temptation. There is good news when you slip and falter. Do not allow the devil to bring in condemnation. He will be quick to seize the opportunity; therefore, you must hold God's word in your heart. "There is now no condemnation for those in Christ" (Romans 8:1). God has made a glorious provision for our failures. "If we confess our sins, he is faithful and righteous to forgive us our sins and to cleanse us from all unrighteousness" (1 John 1:9). Ask God to forgive you, and take Him at His word. He is good for it!

You will discover an inner struggle likened to a raging war. This conflict will be the new man and the Holy Spirit doing battle with your unredeemed humanity. As you grow, develop, and mature, you will discover an inner strengthening of the new creature. You will experience greater power in saying no to sinful desires and pleasures that reside within your fallen humanity as you experience the resurrection power of Jesus Christ.

Learning, discovering, accepting, and acting upon who and what you have become in Christ will be a progressive journey. Paul placed it all in perspective for us in his letter to the Colossians. "To whom God willed to make known what is the riches of the glory of this mystery among the Gentiles, which is Christ in you, the hope of glory" (Colossians 1:27). When the Holy Spirit enters the believer in the new birth, His immediate work of developing Christ within becomes His mission. You will begin to see things differently in the context of right and wrong as you follow His command to put on "the mind of Christ" (1 Corinthians 2:16). The way you view certain issues and thoughts will take on a new perspective as you grow in the sanctification process. You will sense and notice inner changes as the Holy Spirit gives you greater insight into truth and the ways of God. He will promote prayer, Bible study, godly living, and produce a desire to seek God. Learn quickly to set aside a scheduled time for daily prayer and Bible reading. As you walk with the Lord, pray, and study His word; you will experience a greater sensitivity to sin, to the Holy Spirit and the will of God.

Much of God's plan for your life will involve His church, which should become one of your top priorities. The recovering addict will need to rearrange his priorities quickly. This will be essential in the quest to overcome. Old priorities must be trashed and set aside for the new. The church is a God ordained and living institution designed as an instrument to bring men to Christ and disciple them for achieving their God appointed purpose. The Christian has been called to possess and reflect the glory of God. Everything the Christian does should be to glorify Him. "Whether, then, you eat or drink or whatever you do, do all to the glory of God" (1 Corinthians 10:31). The church can be viewed from three different perspectives: the visible church consisting of all professing Christianity, the true church consisting of those who have truly been born again, and the local church defined as a group of believers in a certain locality. It's imperative to understand this fact; not all who profess to be Christians are genuine. You will discover this as you participate and become involved in church activities and missions.

Don't expect to find the perfect church filled with perfect people. The perfect church does not exist, because it's made up of imperfect people. Spiritual growth and maturity will require fellowship with a local church. Every Christian is undergoing spiritual growth as they progress in God's prescribed method. God's word instructs the child of God to be involved in the local church with this exhortation. "Not forsaking our own assembling together, as is the habit of some, but encouraging one another; and all the more as you see the day drawing near" (Hebrews 10:25). Once you become a child of God, your lifestyle will need to include faithful church attendance, membership and participation in spiritual activities. This will have a tremendous impact upon God's general and specific will for your life.

Church is not an option for the Christian. Membership, participation, and attendance are imperative, as well as a command of God. This is God's prescribed method and means of worship. The local church is a place to praise, worship, serve, learn, grow and spiritually develop. God has established a place in the church for each of His children to serve. To neglect faithful membership in a local church is to ignore the command of God's word. This should be one of the primary activities of a true and faithful born-again child of God. The church is where you will learn to serve God, serve others, study, and mature in "the faith that was once for all handed down to the saints" (Jude 1:3).

God has gifted and talented you with purpose. He has blessed you with gifts and talents that will become meaningful blessings to the church, as you pursue God's command to serve others. Your purpose is to become an instrumental tool in the hand of God. He desires to use you in leading and helping others find the life and freedom you will discover.

Through the word of God, the church, and the Holy Spirit, Jesus Christ will lead you toward restoration and recovery. He will call you away from the sin that once sought to destroy you. The Holy Spirit will eventually use you to reach out and become a tool in ministering to others who need God's help. God's Addiction Recovery Plan on The Biblical Path to Freedom leads the addict to this fact: **I must accept by faith the assurance of a new birth, and understand I am a new creature with a divine nature.**

Chapter 7

Free To Live Clean

Freedom Step Six

I must understand Jesus Christ has set me free, and given me the power to live a clean life.

John 8:36
"So if the Son makes you free, you will be free indeed."

Romans 8:11
"But if the Spirit of Him who raised Jesus from the dead dwells in you, He who raised Christ Jesus from the dead will also give life to your mortal bodies through His Spirit who dwells in you."

Ephesians 3:20
"Now to Him who is able to do far more abundantly beyond all that we ask or think, according to the power that works within us."

We previously learned that all men without Christ are spiritual slaves to sin, overpowered and mastered by Satan. When an individual truly accepts Jesus Christ as Lord and Savior, God becomes his new Master. The redeemed becomes a "slave of righteousness" (Romans 6:18), rather than remaining captivated by unrighteousness and being enslaved to the bondage of his addiction. The genuine Christian will have a heart's desire to obey God and live righteously. The new nature has a propensity and yearning to do what is right. God has set the believer free from sin's ownership and Christ has broken the chain of Satan's mastery. The born-again believer is no longer obligated to obey Satan. God has spiritually redeemed the believer and broken the chains of sin holding him captive.

The "law of sin and of death" (Romans 8:2) no longer owns the person who has come to Christ. The believer is now free to live as God's word declares he should. To taste real freedom is to experience the power and ability to live the way God created, designed, and intended. He has blessed His children with the Holy Spirit, provided them the written word of God and the church to help them along their journey of faith. The very power that raised Jesus Christ from the dead now works in the believer's earthen vessel. God has set us up to overcome by empowering the believer to "overwhelmingly conquer through Him" (Romans 8:37). The Holy Spirit provides the believer with the power to live right, to do His will, to obey Him, and live under the dictates of God's word.

The Christian is free to live and walk in the will of God. True freedom is the ability or capacity to live as God commands. God desires all men to become members of His kingdom and walk in newness of life. Kingdom living is defined as "righteousness, and peace, and joy in the Holy Spirit" (Romans 8:37). This is the abundant life God offers to all who will call upon Him with childlike faith. He requires us to submit our lives to Him unconditionally and without reservation.

To be righteous is to have a right relationship with God. We cannot reiterate enough; righteousness can only be acquired by faith in the accomplished work of Jesus Christ on the cross. Jesus lived a perfect life without sin and gave His life on the cross as a substitute for sinful man's offense. He took our sin upon Himself and in turn offers us His righteousness. Man needs the righteousness of Christ if he is to have a right relationship with God. Once an individual has been born again, he is justified and right with God. This is an important fact for the new born Christian to understand and accept. It's imperative for the Christian to understand who and what he has become. "He made Him who knew no sin to be sin on our behalf, so that we might become the righteousness of God in Him" (2 Corinthians 5:21). The Christian should come to see himself as "the righteousness of God," for Christ has made and declared the believer to be righteous. The child of God may not always feel or act righteous, but when God declares a man righteous, he becomes the righteousness of God in Christ.

Divine peace comes in conjunction with a right relationship to God. Understanding who and what we are in Christ is essential to experiencing and maintaining God's blessed peace. The apostle Paul speaks of a marvelous peace that is available to those who know Christ and place their burdens at His feet. "And the peace of God, which surpasses all comprehension, will guard your hearts and your minds in Christ Jesus" (Philippians 4:7). Biblical Christianity and faith are not "pie in the sky religion" as some would suggest. The truth can be tasted, felt, smelled, heard, seen, experienced, lived, and enjoyed. This peace that God affords has been experienced by millions throughout the age of Christ and His church. It's a glorious experience beyond explanation. It comes by knowing and trusting Him who is sovereign over all things. As His children, "we know that God causes all things to work together for good to those who love God, to those who are called according to His purpose" (Romans 8:28). Those who have been born again can accept the precious promises of God and stand upon them by faith, rather than living on feelings and emotions. To be right with God and walk in His peace that surpasses understanding is one of the great and glorious privileges of a true walk with the risen Christ.

God gives great joy to those who will follow His precepts. People of the world generally live as if they were constantly riding a roller coaster. Life for many is filled with ups and downs based upon feelings, emotions, circumstances and situations. Most people live their entire lives based upon their emotional state at any given moment. When unpleasant circumstances or situations strike, people become down, depressed, and sometimes despondent. When pleasant circumstances or situations return, they are once again elated, happy, and back on top of the world. The eternal joy God provides His children is not affected by situations and circumstances, for God's joy within the heart of man is steadfast. It's always there regardless of what one may be facing. God provides His children with emotional and mental stability as they live in the midst of an unstable world. The love of God is able to dispel fear from the heart of a believer. Paul writes to Timothy, "For God has not given us a spirit of timidity, but of power and love and discipline" (2 Timothy 1:7). Kingdom living affords kingdom joy and peace to those who will submit their lives to Jesus Christ. The believer has been empowered to live a life of freedom and no longer has to live in fear of God's judgment. He has a great and glorious future ahead of him.

One of the greatest challenges of an addict is learning to face the obstacles of life without alcohol or drugs. God empowers His people to face those challenges. He has made them over-comers in the midst of a world running in the wrong direction. The ways of the world are contrary to the will, purpose, and plan of God. There is no greater enjoyment in life than to be filled with God's righteousness, peace, joy and power. Life can be meaningful and purposeful when we set our feet upon the right path. The Psalmist illustrated this way with precision when he wrote, "Your word is a lamp to my feet and a light to my path" (Psalms 119:105).

Many of God's people live defeated lives because they do not know and understand who they are in Christ. Biblical Christianity is much more than dead religion and ritualistic exercise. All religion outside of genuine Christianity is bankrupt, part of the world system, and resides in a state of spiritual death. The spiritual transformation of a Christian is attributed to God imputing His righteousness and embedding His divine nature within the believer. This metamorphosis is essential and will produce strength, power, understanding and insight as it grows and develops. The believer must learn to be aware and alert of his surroundings at all times.

The new believer will quickly discover an enemy is running loose and continually stalking God's people. The recovering addict will be no exception to the rule. The Christian will be confronted by an enemy of whom Peter so aptly describes and defines. "Your adversary, the devil, prowls around like a roaring lion, seeking someone to devour" (1 Peter 5:8). Satan is a literal and formidable foe, a fallen angel in rebellion against God. He was known as Lucifer before he rebelled and became Satan. (Isaiah 14:12). He led an angelic rebellion against God and brought about man's fall in the Garden of Eden. This evil creature hates God and despises all who are members of His family. He hates all men because God loves us and we were created in His image. His desire is to defeat God, defeat you, and destroy God's plan. He has already lost the battle, his fate is sealed, and only time stands between him and his doom.

Jesus defined Satan as a thief who "comes only to steal and kill and destroy" (John 10:10). He will seize every opportunity to create problems for those who seek to obey and follow Christ. When Jesus was confronted by

Satan, He used the word of God to defeat him. The Christian who walks with Christ must always keep in mind this important fact. "You are from God, little children, and have overcome them; because greater is He who is in you than he who is in the world" (1 John 4:4). If you have truly received Christ as your personal Lord and Savior, the greatest power in the universe resides within your earthen vessel.

The letter to the Hebrews gives great assurance to the people of God. "I will never desert you, nor will I ever forsake you" (Hebrews 13:5). God will stand with His people in whatever circumstances they encounter. He will see the recovering addict through the trials, struggles and challenges he faces. Though the addict may stumble and fall, the promise and faithfulness of God will always be there to help him rise back to his feet. He is far greater and powerful than Satan who is defined as "the god of this world" (2 Corinthians 4:4). Although he may be the "god of this world," he is not the god of a Christian. Provided you have truly received Jesus Christ, He is now in control of your life and will see you through until the end of time as we know it. "For I am confident of this very thing, that He who began a good work in you will perfect it until the day of Christ Jesus" (Philippians 1:6). God always completes what He begins. The work He has begun in His children will come to fruition in accordance with His will. God cannot fail!

As we will explore in a later chapter, the child of God is completely and eternally secure in Christ. Once an individual becomes a child of God, the word of God sets forth another precious promise.

> But in all these things we overwhelmingly conquer through Him who loved us. For I am convinced that neither death, nor life, nor angels, nor principalities, nor things present, nor things to come, nor powers, nor height, nor depth, nor any other created thing, will be able to separate us from the love of God, which is in Christ Jesus (Romans 8:37-39).

God loves His children with an unconditional love. Regardless of what may happen in your life as a Christian; remember, God is sovereign and in control of all things. He is able to take every circumstance and situation in your life and work it out for your good. This is a biblical fact you need to accept and tenaciously hold on too. Faith in the facts will become a tremendous asset in helping you learn to trust Christ, regardless of what may happen along the journey.

Assuming you have accepted Jesus Christ as Lord and Savior, God has adopted you into His family as a lifetime member. Once you're in, there is absolutely no way out! You have been blessed and afforded with all the benefits and privileges of being a child of God. These benefits and privileges will be discovered as you pursue walking an upright life before God, who provides man with the only eternal security system ever developed. Jesus says you are now free. What are you free from, and what are you free to do?

You must understand that salvation in Jesus Christ defines you as being free from "the law of sin and of death" (Romans 8:2). Earlier we learned the "wages of sin, is death" (Romans 3:23). Man is spiritually dead before coming to Christ. Upon receiving Christ, a man is spiritually resurrected from the dead and given new life. This spiritual resurrection will one day result in the resurrection of a new body to be inhabited by the new creature. It will be the same type of body Jesus possessed after His physical resurrection from the dead. It is defined as a glorified body. "Just as we have born the image of the earthy, we will also bear the image of the heavenly" (1 Corinthians 15:49). We now live in an earthly body designed to reside on earth; however, we will one day possess a heavenly body fitted for heaven and eternity. This promise of a new body in future glorification is assured by God. The new divine creature can never again be threatened with spiritual death. You should understand, eternal life is both a present and yet a future possession. The new body will not be subject to death, disease, sickness, or sorrow. Jesus said, "I am the resurrection and the life; he who believes in me will live even if he dies, and everyone who lives and believes in Me will never die" (John 25-26).

Unless you are one of those who are alive in the first phase of His second coming, your current physical body will experience death. The Bible does not define physical death as a cessation of existence. Those who physically die in Christ, immediately ascend to be with God. The believer will join others who know Christ in a sinless Paradise called heaven. To be free from the "law of sin and death" (Romans 8:2), means sin and death no longer have power over you.

Sin and death were crucified on the cross of Calvary when Christ hung in your place. You will discover your unredeemed humanity will cause conflict and problems in this life. As a result, you will never be completely without sin on this side of eternity. However, there is good news in Christ, for sin can no longer impose the penalty of death; you have been set free from the law.

This does not suggest sin will be without consequences. Sin in the life of a Christian will be dealt with by a loving Heavenly Father. He will discipline His children as necessary. "For those whom the Lord loves He disciplines" (Hebrews 12:6). There are always natural consequences of sin, as well as consequences to be determined by God's sovereign control and judgment. The consequences of a believer's sins will be determined by God. The judgment of a believer will never be spiritual death or punishment. God provides us adequate assurance when His word advises us of this fact: "therefore, there is now no condemnation for those who are in Christ Jesus" (Romans 8:1). Only those who are living outside a relationship with Christ are subject to the law's condemnation. Christians have been set free from condemnation, and presently possesses eternal life which can never be lost, forfeited or destroyed by anyone.

John, one of the closest disciples to Jesus wrote, "these things have I written to you who believe in the name of the Son of God, so that you may know that you have eternal life" (1 John 5:13). Many such precious promises of God can be found in His word. You must find these promises, allow them to take root in the heart, and cherish them as golden nuggets of truth. The wisdom and knowledge of God's word is unending and never runs dry. You will need to hide these nuggets of truth in your heart. They will rise to the surface when needed to invoke faith, confidence, courage, strength, boldness and encouragement. Paul wrote, "Faith comes from hearing, and hearing by the word of Christ" (Romans 10:17). Spending time in the word of God is imperative to the growth and development of your faith. Taking hold of God's precious promises by faith and making practical application will bring consistent victory, joy, peace and righteousness to the Christian experience.

God has a marvelous plan and purpose for your life. His design means to make your life meaningful and worthwhile. As you discover His plan and walk in it with the help of the Holy Spirit, life will become increasingly meaningful.

You will discover living does not have to be a futile effort of existence. Man was created for God's pleasure. If God created man for His pleasure, and man insists on living in rebellion, he will never have the capacity to please God. A life of disobedience is never content, satisfied or fulfilled. These blessings can only be experienced as a result of an obedient lifestyle. How does one please God? It is impossible for a sinner who does not know Christ to please God. The sinner does not have the capacity, desire or power to please God. He is in bondage to sin and incapable of doing what God requires of those who would please Him. This is not the case for those who have the resurrected Christ living within. In Christ, man finds freedom from sin's bondage and the law's penalty. The Christian has been blessed with the freedom to obey God. He has been empowered by the Holy Spirit to live a life of righteousness, holiness, and obedience.

The world does not and cannot understand such freedom. A worldly person defines freedom as the capacity to do as he pleases. Freedom for the sinner is fulfilling every wanton desire of his sinful nature; he believes in the message of "living and letting live." Those who are born of the world are bound by sinful corruption. There are two great illustrations defining why a sinner acts and behaves as he does. Consider two of God's beautiful creations in the animal kingdom: the cat and the dog. What cat does not have the inner desire to stalk a bird or lizard? What dog does not have the inclination to chase after a cat or squirrel? It's an ingrained desire of the nature they are born with. Is it possible for a man to change the internal nature of a cat or a dog? "Can the Ethiopian change his skin or the leopard his spots" (Jeremiah 13:23)? The obvious answer is no. Neither does the cat or dog have the capacity to change its own nature. Man may be able to suppress the actions of a cat or dog by threat of punishment, but he is incapable of changing an animal's internal instinct, and the same is true of man. Prisons, mental wards, jails, hospitals and graveyards are filled with victims of the sinful nature. Those who found themselves unable to subdue or suppress their sinful desires ended up doing something stupid and suffered the consequences. Something arose up within them at some given moment causing them to snap. That something is a sinful nature that resides within all at the moment of conception.

Like the cat or dog, man is unable to set himself free or change the sinful corruption of his personhood. His entire personality has been affected by his corrupted nature. Man is born sinful at the core of his being and sins because he is a sinner. Unless his sinful state is eradicated, he will depart this world in an eternal state of sinfulness. Men in their sinful condition are completely unacceptable to God, and corruption cannot be allowed in a place of perfection. One rotten apple in a barrel will destroy the entire harvest if not disposed of. God cannot accept sin in His eternal residence of glory. The sinful nature does not have the capacity to be made acceptable to God; therefore, it must be destroyed. The sinful state of man is like a progressive disease. It's comparable to the addict who is being destroyed by his addiction, which only serves as a symptom of his sin sickened soul. It continues to grow and degenerate into something worthless and useless. Man is spiritually sick, and desperately needs the healing that is available only in Christ. The prophet Isaiah speaks of man's spiritual disease and the cure available.

> But He was pierced through for our transgressions, He was crushed for our iniquities; the chastening for our well-being fell upon Him, and by His scourging we are healed. All of us like sheep have gone astray, each of us has turned to his own way; but the Lord has caused the iniquity of us all to fall on Him (Isaiah 53:5-6).

Modern day philosophers, psychiatrists, and psychologists attempt to convince man he is basically a good creature. Worldly counsel advises man he needs to find himself and have a greater self-esteem. He needs to think more highly of himself and understand his value. They teach a man must see himself as good and acceptable. This philosophy runs completely contrary with the teachings of Jesus Christ and the word of God. "Blessed are the poor in spirit, for theirs is the kingdom of heaven" (Matthew 5:3). God insists that man recognize himself as a wretched sinner who possesses no righteousness of his own. Man is brought into this world as sinful, rotten, wretched, no good, and corrupted by sin. "For all of us have become like one who is unclean, and all our righteous deeds are like a filthy garment" (Isaiah 64:6). Man is unable and utterly incapable of redeeming himself; he is spiritually dead, and dead men can do nothing. Only God can raise the dead and the spiritually dead need a spiritual resurrection. Man may be able to reform himself to some extent, but to change his own nature and do good as defined by God is an utter impossibility. Only a divine supernatural act of God can change the sinful nature of man into a nature of divine holiness and righteousness. This is what God does for those who truly accept and believe on Jesus Christ.

Satan will make every attempt to keep you from enjoying the life of freedom inherited in Jesus Christ. He will seek to rob you of the joy, peace, and righteousness of an obedient lifestyle by luring you into disobedience with temptation and false promises. His lies will suggest nothing has really happened. He will scream and whisper that you have been deceived by false hope. He will say it's all a fairy tale from the Land of Oz and a wild imagination in your mind. The devils will attempt to convince you of God's contempt by constantly reminding you of your past. Darkness will seek to cloud your mind with thoughts that suggest God will never forgive you of all your guilt. He will attempt to convince you that you have finally lost your mind and become one of those religious fanatics. Satan and his imps will stop at nothing to prevent you from coming to understand who and what you are in Jesus Christ. You must always bear in mind; the enemy's greatest weapon is a lie. This would perhaps explain why addicts are such great liars. Lying is a powerful tool of deception and Satan is a master deceiver. A lie believed will cause men to do things they would not normally do. The addict is often guilty of buying, believing, and swallowing the lies of the world, Satan, and himself.

Jesus described Satan as "the father of lies" (John 8:44). If he can convince you of a lie, he can lead you into one of his many snares. When you dare to stand against him with steadfast confidence and faith, Satan will never destroy your sense of spiritual security. He can lead you astray by feeding you poisonous lies. He will bring up your past and present sins in an attempt to have you believe God is a liar. This was his tactic in the garden when he deceived Eve. With great deception he will seek to convince you God has not performed any internal change. You must forever trust the word of God as truth that cannot be broken. Jesus said, "Heaven and earth will pass away, but My words will not pass away" (Luke 21:33). God's word is trustworthy, and though all else may fail, His word will stand the test of eternity.

Here you find the essence of faith, the practice of believing what God says despite the lies of a deceptive and accusatory enemy. Faith is able to look beyond situations and circumstances which taunt us with seemingly impassible obstacles. "Now faith is the assurance of things hoped for, the conviction of things not seen" (Hebrews 11:1). You will discover this new journey is a life of faith, an adventurous walk with God. It will be an experience which grows with anticipation as to what God has in store for the days, weeks, months, and years ahead. God will sometimes move in special ways and often at unexpected times. You will stand in awe and rest in such promises as, "eye has not seen and ear has not heard, and which have not entered the heart of man, all that God has prepared for those who love Him" (2 Corinthians 2:9). Faith will bring you to accept, believe, and claim special nuggets of truth as you glean faithful facts from God's word.

A great illustration of this faith business is displayed by three train cars. There is an engine, a box car, and a caboose. The engine is representative of facts, the box car is symbolic of faith, and the caboose is illustrative of feelings. Facts, faith, and feelings are three important aspects of man's person. The Christian must learn to maintain each of these elements in their proper perspective, and keep them in order at all times. This is the path and pattern you must walk in your new-found Christian life. Fact must be the power driving the train; faith must follow the facts, and feelings must always take up the rear position. Failure to maintain their proper order can create spiritual schizophrenia. The Bible contains all the facts you need and is sufficient in addressing all the issues of life. God's word is the absolute truth, "the whole truth, and nothing but the truth." The facts of life can be found in the pages of God's written word from Genesis to Revelation. Jesus Christ is the living Word of God, while the Bible is His written word. Biblical facts are the engine empowering the train of life for the Christian, and faith must be placed in those facts alone. If God's word proclaims it, you can place your confidence, hope, and trust in it as a fact. Feelings must take up the rear of the train and follow after faith in the facts. Maintaining a proper perspective on fact, faith, and feeling, will be instrumental in your emotional and mental stability. Many people are guilty of living on feelings and attempting to empower life through emotion, rather than having faith in the facts as revealed in God's word. Beware, this mentality is found in some religious circles and is a recipe for confusion as the facts advise us, "God is not a God of confusion but of peace" (1 Corinthians 14:33). Feelings can be confusing; faith in the facts will stabilize.

Feelings are not always a reliable source, and are not always based on fact. They can be deceptive, misleading, and serve to promote emotional instability. Those who live by feelings tend to ride the roller coaster of life. Such an individual will find themselves up today when the feelings are good and down tomorrow when the feelings plummet. One of the great keys to experiencing the freedom a Christian has received in Christ is learning to "walk by faith, not by sight" (2 Corinthians 5:7). God's word is filled with promises which have not been seen or come to past. On the other hand, God's word is filled with promises known as prophecies which have been fulfilled and serve to demonstrate the faithfulness of God. You must learn to rely and trust upon the word of God. It should become your guiding rule for every endeavor, decision, word and action. Cling to the promises and facts of God's word with tenacity, hiding them in your heart, mind, and soul.

Learn to rest and rely upon the faithfulness of God's word, instead of leaning toward feeling and emotion. Feelings can be manipulated by internal and external circumstances. Simply not feeling well physically can affect the way you feel as a whole. Pound your big toe with a hammer and your entire being will be affected. A difficult situation or circumstance can have great impact upon your feelings. When you learn to walk by faith in the facts and promises of God's word, the feelings will be much easier to accommodate. As the Christian learns to walk by faith and stand on the word of God, his emotions and feelings will be positively affected. God's word must be the controlling factor of your life, if you are to experience the fullness of victory available. You must be constantly on the alert against allowing feelings to dictate your walk. They can slip in and overcome quickly. You may not always feel like getting out of bed, but there are times when you must force yourself up to accomplish a necessary task. This is a major area of life that Satan has mastered; he knows how to manipulate your feelings and is capable of inducing certain emotions. He is deceptive enough to bring tears to your eyes and goose bumps to your flesh. Placing feelings first will lead you off the beaten path of victory. God intends for you to live, think and act based upon the facts of His word, rather than by the way you feel. This is called living and walking by faith. Emotion can be a dangerous motivator, and is often a favorite playground of the enemy. The recovering addict will experience a multitude of feelings and emotions throughout the recovery process. Yielding to feelings and emotions can be another recipe for undue trouble.

There are six primary ways of building up your faith: Bible study, faithful church attendance, reading biblically sound materials, obedience, prayer, and fellowship with other believers. These will be essential practices in developing and maintaining the power of living a lifestyle of freedom in Jesus Christ. A wise recovering addict will package the time once wasted on riotous living, and invest it in building up his faith. If you have followed through on freedom step six, you should be well on the way in The Biblical Path to Freedom. You have been set free and are no longer captive to "the law of sin and death" (Romans 8:2). God's Addiction Recovery Plan leads the addict to this fact: **I must understand Jesus Christ has set me free, and given me the power to live a clean life.**

Chapter 8
Yielding To The Master

Freedom Step Seven

I must turn over and surrender control of my life to Jesus Christ by letting go of my own ambitions, dreams, and desires.

Matthew 16:25
"For whoever wishes to save his life will lose it; but whoever loses his life for My sake will find it."

John 12:25
"He who loves his life loses it; and he who hates his life in this world shall keep it to eternal life."

Mark 8:34
"If anyone wishes to come after Me, he must deny himself, and take up his cross and follow Me."

Hopefully you have taken the prescribed step four of repenting and receiving Jesus Christ as your Lord and Savior? You have left the slave field of sin and entered into the realm of righteousness, where Christ is your new Master. Upon taking step four, an individual is no longer their own, but under the authority, ownership, and management of Jesus Christ. Total surrender is of necessity if you have invited Christ into your life. If you have not totally surrendered in asking Christ into your life, you should pause and purpose to do so. Giving your life to Christ is not a mere intellectual acknowledgement of His existence. Receiving Christ is a complete surrender of your life to Him as Lord. Man must come to God under the terms He has prescribed. God makes no deals and cannot be manipulated. Man does not have the option of coming to Christ by his own means and conditions. Man's own terms are unacceptable to God. He must come to God on His terms, or he will be denied access. The Bible teaches that God is sovereign over all things. He is Almighty, and nothing is beyond His reach or control. When you accept Jesus Christ as Lord and Savior, you become a child of God. Scripture defines those without Christ as children of the devil. "By this the children of God and the children of the devil are obvious: anyone who does not practice righteousness is not of God, nor the one who does not love his brother" (1John 3:10). Paul refers to those without Christ as "children of wrath" (Ephesians 2:3). God is the Christian's Heavenly Father, and He loves His children beyond their capacity to fully comprehend.

He has designed a plan for each of us; whereas we discover the abundant life God has promised. You must learn to trust and rely upon Him in all the issues of life. It's imperative that you allow Him to be the bus driver and manager. This is accomplished by trusting and loving Him with all your heart, mind, and soul (Matthew 22:37). Your desire should be toward following and obeying God in all things. He is now in control of the situations and circumstances of the journey you will travel. He will be overseer, supervisor, and manager in all aspects of your life. He has already traveled the road ahead of you and prepared the way. God is good for His word and has promised to work all things out for our good when we follow Him (Romans 8:28). You must place all your interests in the hands of a sovereign God by asking and allowing Him to work out His perfect will in your life. This will require a submissive attitude which requires letting go of your own ambitions, dreams, desires, and wishes.

Your primary goal should be to please God, seek His plan, purpose and will. God has a specific and general will for His children. His general will is the same for everyone, and can be found in the written word of God. The Bible should become the authority by which you live and conduct yourself. It should be used as a rule to measure, judge, and discern all things. Discovering the general will of God will require quality time reading and studying the Bible on a regular basis. As you study His word, it will be written upon your heart, and rest upon your mind as a guide. The Holy Spirit will lead you through the word of God as to His general will. In addition to God's general will, He has a specific plan designed for you, with the expressed purpose of producing a fruitful life. You are a unique individual; there is only one of you. Only you can fulfill the purpose and plan for which you were designed.

Consider a working piece of machinery and how it operates. Each part of the machine is designed to fulfill its proper role in bringing about its functioning purpose. God is actively involved in His purpose and plan. He is building a kingdom that will exist for eternity. In this kingdom, everyone will have their proper place and position. The Christian is a member of God's kingdom and has a specific role in its proper function and proliferation. God created and designed you with purpose. True fulfillment is discovered living within His general and specific will. Paul likens the church to a physical body with different parts such as eyes, hands, and ears. He writes, "For the body is not one member, but many" (1 Corinthians 12:14). God has a unique role for you to fill in His kingdom. Each part of the human body has its proper role and function. This is true also with the body of Christ. Each child of God is a member of the body and has his proper role in building the kingdom.

The obvious question is how do I discover God's specific purpose for me? This is one the most common questions of a new Christian. God's specific will is discovered in following after His general will. You must always remember that God is in control of all things. Once you become faithful in following and obeying the general will of God as found in His written word, He will arrange the circumstances and situations to bring about His specific purpose. A great prayer of submission is, "Lord, do whatever is necessary to get me where I should be at any given moment in time." Herein is found the great elements of faith and trust! When you follow His general will, He will lead you into His specific will. Walking with God is a daily journey filled with anticipation and expectation. The Christian must always keep in mind that he is to follow God's timing. Remember, God is the driver; you're just along for the ride. When you follow His general will and instruction, God will make sure you arrive at His scheduled destination on time. This is an issue of trust, faith, confidence, and complete reliance upon His sovereign control. The Christian's responsibility is to obey and follow as God leads. The bus may decide to wait at the stop for a while; it may move forward at a fast or slow pace, and may back up on occasion. You must not seek to take control or drive the bus yourself. Leave the driving to God! When the Hebrews were led out of Egypt and into the wilderness on their journey toward the promise land, God led them at His own pace and timing.

> The Lord was going before them in a pillar of cloud by day to lead them on the way, and in a pillar of fire by night to give them light, that they might travel by day and by night. He did not take away the pillar of cloud by day, nor the pillar of fire by night, from before the people (Exodus 14:21-22).

Under the new covenant, Christians live in the church age. There is no "pillar of cloud by day, nor a pillar of fire by night" to follow. God replaced the pillar and cloud by giving us Jesus Christ, the Holy Spirit, and His written word. Learning to discern the voice of God is a process and learning experience. The prophet Isaiah speaks to us regarding the voice of God. "Your ears will hear a word behind you saying, "this is the way, walk in it," whenever you turn to the right or to the left" (Isaiah 30:21). As the believer studies the word of God and tunes in with the voice of the Spirit, he will learn to know God's voice and recognize His leading. You must pray and live the words of Jesus as He prayed in the Garden of Gethsemane, "not as I will, but as you will" (Matthew 26:39). It's essential to get alone with God on a regular basis. This should a special time to be practiced in a place of quietness and serenity. The Psalmist exhorts God's people to "Be still, and know that I am God" (Psalm 46:10 KJV).

Submission to the will of God is the ultimate key to victory in Christ. The greatest priority in your life should be whatever God desires. Discovering God's general will, begins with spending quality time in His written word. What does a new born baby need to grow, develop, and mature? The new born infant needs a sufficient amount of milk. Peter exhorts the child of God, "Like new born babies, long for the pure milk of the word, so that by it you may grow in respect to salvation" (1 Peter 2:2). The new born man longs to be fed the word of God. As a child develops it also needs solid food to continue in growth and maturity. "But solid food is for the mature, who because of practice have their senses trained to discern good and evil (Hebrews 5:14). The same is true for spiritual infants as well as mature adults. Every born- again believer needs a regular diet of milk and meat from the word of God.

The Christian has called upon Christ and surrendered control to Him. He has made you clean and declared you righteous in your relationship with Him. He will begin His normal practice of cleaning you up within, a process known as progressive sanctification. This is a supernatural internal program by which God starts and continues to purge our lives from those things not pleasing to Him. Some areas may require intense surgery, while others may require a bandage. God began construction of the new creature from the moment you were born again. To be sanctified is to be set apart by God and for His purposes. He will prompt and require you to separate yourself from impurities, vileness, and other traits unacceptable to Him.

God's building project takes place in the inner most part of our person. Jesus Christ is a masterful carpenter and extremely proficient in His work, who completes what He begins. In displaying the faithfulness of God, Paul writes, "For I am confident of this very thing, that He who began a good work in you will perfect it until the day of Christ Jesus" (Philippians 1:6). Rest assured with confidence, God is going to complete what He has begun in you. He will be working even in those moments when you are not aware. It may seem painful and unpleasant at times. Change rarely comes easy for any of us, and is one of the most difficult processes we experience. We are seldom comfortable with change because it removes us from our comfort zone. As a patient must yield to the surgeon's knife and trust His ability to complete the surgery, the child of God must trust the Great Physician who gained control when He entered the surgical room.

The Christian should desire nothing less than the work and purpose for which God has predestined him. What God wills must be at the forefront of our priorities. You have a new foundation for Christ to build upon. God may allow you to continue in your current position, career, and status, or He may determine to lead you in a completely new direction, away from your past and current interests. He may call you to be a witness in your existing workplace, or He may decide to move you into another field of employment. He could possibly call you into part-time or full-time ministry. Your life is in the hands of a loving Heavenly Father who knows what is best. God understands what will truly fulfill and satisfy your heart. He has designed you with purpose and the ultimate fulfillment in life is progressing forward in His plan. The prophet Jeremiah tells the story of a potter and his clay. According to the master plan, God is the Potter and we are the clay. Always keep that in mind; it is God who molds, kneads, and shapes us into what He desires. The clay cannot tell the potter when and how to perform his task of fashioning and completing his work. The clay must never attempt to tell the potter how to run his business. It is the potter who determines what the clay will be. The responsibility of the clay is yielding to the potter and allowing him to work until his product is completed. The Christian must yield to the Master Potter's hands if he is to become all that God has planned.

> The word which came to Jeremiah from the Lord saying, "Arise and go down to the potter's house, and there I will announce My words to you." Then, I went down to the potter's house, and there he was, making something on the wheel. But the vessel that he was making of clay was spoiled in the hand of the potter; so he remade it into another vessel, as it pleased the potter to make. Then the word of the LORD came to me saying, "Can I not, O house of Israel, deal with you as this potter does, declares the LORD. Behold, like the clay in the potter's hand, so are you in My hand, O house of Israel" (Jeremiah 18:1-6).

Perhaps you had great plans when you entered the potter's house. Those plans must now be set aside in humble submission to the potter. God's Spirit and the word of God will direct and order your steps. "In all your ways acknowledge Him, and He will make your paths straight" (Proverbs 3:6). Speaking of those "born of the Spirit" (John 3:6), Jesus said, "The wind blows where it wishes and you hear the sound of it, but do not know where it comes from and where it is going; so is everyone who is born of the Spirit" (John 3:8). The born-again believer would do well to consider the flight of a feather in the wind. Where does the feather travel? What is the feather's destiny? Is the feather or the wind in control? The feather has no control as to where the wind takes its flight; it must yield to the wind as its driving force. So, it is with those who yield to the Spirit of God. The Holy Spirit will lead and take care of where and when you need to go. The key is yielding and believing that He will control the wind as you yield to His general will and purpose. He is the Master of the wind who will open and close appropriate doors if you will step aside and allow Him.

The Old Testament character Abraham was confronted by God, told to pack his bags and leave his country. He was commanded to leave his relatives behind, to leave Ur, and follow as God would lead. He was not told what his destination would be. Abraham stepped out in faith and obeyed God. Now the LORD said to Abram, "Go forth from your country, and from your relatives and from your father's house, to the land which I will show you" (Genesis 12:1). Abraham faced many difficult challenges when he stepped out by faith and obeyed God. When he obeyed, he discovered God was faithful to go with him, and see him through each trial. Abraham "was looking for the city which foundations, whose architect and builder is God" (Hebrews 11:10). What Abraham chose to leave behind could not compare to what was being prepared. One of the greatest prayers you can ever pray with sincerity is asking God to do whatever is necessary to make sure you're in His perfect will. This is a prayer of submission in yielding your destiny and fate to a loving and faithful God who is looking out for your best interests. Perhaps you have had the misfortune of having someone forsake you in times past? God promises to never let us down or forsake us. God has given His people a steadfast promise that has withstood the test of time, and His promises can be stood upon with absolute assurance. "I will never desert you, nor will I ever forsake you, so that we confidently say, The Lord is my helper, I will not be afraid" (Hebrews 13:5).

This is another one of those golden nuggets of truth found in God's word. The Christian must learn to cling to these factual promises when facing trials and testing. This is one of the areas spoken of earlier in the train illustration of fact, faith and feelings. The Christian will not always feel like God is with him. You may sin and miss the mark of God's general will for your life in some area. Immediately, the enemy will move in to taunt and suggest that God has forsaken you, and you may indeed feel as if He has. The Christian must never forget; Jesus defined Satan as "the father of lies" (John 8:44). The enemy of your soul will seek to manipulate your feelings and emotions in times of trouble. When facing times of difficulty, the enemy will seek to cast doubt upon God's faithfulness. The Christian must hold to the promise of God, regardless of what may come. The enemy is effective at hurling men into pity parties. There is but one effective weapon in fending off the fiery darts of the enemy. Paul writes, "In addition to all, taking up the shield of faith with which you will be able to extinguish all the flaming arrows of the evil one" (Ephesians 6:16). As a child of God, you're continually involved in a spiritual war with battles raging all around. You have become a soldier in God's army. With growth and maturity, the warfare will become more intense. God will train and prepare you for each battle to be waged. The enemy wants you sidelined and AWOL (absent without leave). His intention is to spiritually wound and incapacitate you. He will diligently work at thrusting you into a pit of despair, and seek to induce old stinky thinking back into your thoughts.

When an addict comes to Christ, the mind is generally filled with stinky thinking from the past. The addict's mind has been trained, formed, and fashioned with a stinky thought process. You must move away from the stinky thinking syndrome that embellishes such thoughts as "I can't." The stinky thinker who says "I can't," is really saying "I will not!" Stinky thinkers love to blame others for their ills. Most addicts are habitual at pointing the finger and blaming others. They have spent years, or even a lifetime living a stinky lifestyle. Stinky thoughts omit God from the equation. Paul in his letter to the Romans exhorts his readers. "Do not be conformed to this world, but be transformed by the renewing of your mind, so that you may prove what the will of God is, that which is good and acceptable and perfect" (Romans 12:2).

Be careful to take special note of Paul's exhortation regarding "the renewing of your mind." All sinners come to Christ with a mind saturated in stinky thinking. The addict seems to have a much greater propensity for rotten thought patterns. The pigpen tends to be a mass producer of sour thought. The mind has been trained and shaped to think according to the world's way of ordering things. These ways can be attributed to the environment we grew up in, the parents who reared us, the school system that educated us, and the mass media of marketing which serves to mold us into various worldly philosophies. God's mold carries us in the very opposite direction. The ways of the world are always running contrary to the ways and will of God.

Man has been programmed to view matters with a worldview rather than a biblical view. Herein we find the reason for untold sufferings. Wisdom advises us, "For as he thinks within himself, so is he" (Proverbs 23:7). Many of man's problems can be attributed to his own way of thinking. When he lives according to his own thoughts and conditioning, rather than listening to God, he is destined for failure. God says we must change our way of thinking and conform our minds to His will. Being conformed to the world's standard of doing things is not the biblical way of freedom. The Christian will live with an ongoing process of learning to think God's way and to live in accordance with His commands. This can only be accomplished in discovering how and what God thinks. A good example of worldly thought verses godly thinking would be Paul's words to the Philippians, "I can do all things through Him who strengthens me" (Philippians 4:13). The addict is inebriated with excuses as to why he cannot accomplish certain tasks. His stinking way of thinking has become a habit of hindrance. This ingrained way of thinking will not dissipate immediately. It will take some time, work, cleansing, patience and prayer. When God tells us to do something, He empowers us to perform it. Jesus spoke these words of encouragement to His disciples; Looking at them, Jesus said, "With people it is impossible, but not with God; for all things are possible with God" (Mark 10:27).

"I cannot" should be stricken from our vocabulary when it comes to God's general and specific will. God does not require the impossible of anyone. When He asks us to do something, He also enables and empowers us to follow through. This does not suggest there will be no difficulty, frustration, or temporary failures in our attempts to behave as God wishes. Changing our way of thinking can be a slow or rapid process. How does the addict change his way of thinking? Simply by following the general will of God. God's word is supernatural and has a changing effect upon those who bathe their minds in it. Saturating the mind and spirit with the word of God is another key to discovering and living the victorious life. Take heed and pay close attention to the word of God in Hebrews. "The word of God is living, and active, and sharper than any two-edged sword" (Hebrews 4:12). In Ephesians, Paul mentions the cleansing element of God's word, "So that he might sanctify her, having cleansed her by the washing of water with the word." (Ephesians 5:26). The word of God is a cleansing agent filled with power to wash away unhealthy thinking. God's word is supernatural in nature; it's not just another book. Speaking of His own words, Jesus said, "It is the Spirit who gives life; the flesh profits nothing; the words that I have spoken to you are spirit and are life" (John 6:63).

The same can be said of the entire word of God from Genesis to Revelation. God's word is powerful and has the power to change your way of thinking by conforming it to the mind and will of Christ. The Christian will never spend an excessive amount of time in the written word. The more time you spend bathing your mind in the cleansing agent of God's word, the more you will sense your thoughts beginning to change. The word of God is powerful and will cleanse your mind of stinky thinking as you allow it to consume you. Choose to pickle you mind with the word of God, rather than in alcohol and drugs. As with anything worth having, sound thinking does not come easy. Victorious living in Christ is an ever-increasing process and experience that requires time, effort, obedience, and diligence.

Spending quality time in the word of God will prove to be an effective means of developing what Paul refers to as "the mind of Christ" (1 Corinthians 2:16). You receive this mind at the moment of spiritual birth. As we related earlier, you can use the illustration of an infant child in helping to understand this important aspect of conversion to Christ. An infant child is born with a worldly mind. The physical mind of a child is under developed and immature. The same is true of a new born spiritual child of God. The spiritual mind must be developed in proper thinking. It must grow, develop, and mature. The word of God and the Holy Spirit will serve us in maturing the mind of Christ within. As the mind of Christ grows, the Christian will discover himself yielding to the will of God more regularly, rather than submitting to his own fleshly desire and ambition. The Christian will eventually begin to think the word of God, rather than dwelling on what the world or his unredeemed humanity suggests. The sinful mind filled with stinky thoughts desires to have its own way. The mind cleansed and transformed by the word of God desires to follow God's thoughts.

When the mind is transformed by the word of God, the Christian begins to see, hear, think, pray, live, behave, and speak with the mind of Christ.

The biblical story of a young rich man is an apt illustration of a man who refused to let go of his own way of thinking. He could not discard his own ambitions and desires. He simply refused to bring himself around and submit to the mind of Christ.

> And someone came to Him and said, "Teacher, what good thing shall I do that I may obtain eternal life?" And He said to him, "Why are you asking Me about what is good? There is only One who is good; but if you wish to enter into life, keep the commandments." Then he said to Him, "Which ones?" And Jesus said, "You shall not commit murder; you shall not commit adultery; you shall not steal; you shall not bear false witness; honor your father and mother; and you shall love your neighbor as yourself." The young man said to Him, "All these things I have kept; what am I still lacking?" Jesus said to him, "If you wish to be complete, go and sell your possessions and give to the poor, and you will have treasure in heaven; and come, follow Me." But when the young man heard this statement, he went away grieving; for he was one who owned much property (Matthew 19:16).

This young man wanted the best of both worlds. He wanted all God had for him, but was not willing to make the ultimate sacrifice of self. He was not willing to let go of his own ambitions, dreams, desires and worldly pleasures. He was unwilling to surrender all of his heart to Christ. His money held a very special place and priority in his heart. Jesus knew this man's heart and confronted him with his poor process of thought. In the end, when he crossed the threshold of eternity, he lost it all. The rich man could hold onto his riches but for so long. Eternal life is a possession that will last forever. Jesus said, "For what does it profit a man to gain the whole world, and forfeit his own soul" (Mark 8:36). Filled with stinky thinking, the rich young ruler held onto his riches and forfeited his eternal soul. The addict must shed his tendency and propensity toward a negative thought process.

Coming to Christ requires a willingness to give up whatever He may ask. The key is a willingness of the heart. Are you willing to do whatever God asks of you? If we truly wish to receive and experience victorious Christian living, we must be willing to lose all we have in order to gain Him. It's a trade-off well worth the costs. The old adage is true, "you cannot take it with you." Have you ever seen a funeral procession with a hearse pulling a trailer filled with money and material possessions? God requires us to forsake anything in our heart that robs Him of His rightful place. He demands to be seated upon the throne of our hearts.

It's a new world, a new way, a complete change of lifestyle. Thinking clearly and acting upon biblical thoughts will lead to clean living. This will bring you to the place of giving up your own life in submission to God's will. The Holy Spirit will assist you in overcoming the unhealthy desires and demands of sin. God's Addiction Recovery Plan and The Biblical Path to Freedom lead the addict to this fact: **I must turn over and surrender control of my life to Jesus Christ by letting go of my own ambitions, dreams, and desires.**

Chapter 9
A Time Of Transition

Freedom Step Eight

I must set aside the old life, and put on the new life I have been given in Jesus Christ.

Ephesians 4:21-24
"If indeed you have heard Him and have been taught in Him, just as the truth is in Jesus, that, in reference to your former manner of life, you lay aside the old self, which is being corrupted in accordance with the lust of deceit, and that you be renewed in the spirit of your mind, and put on the new self, which in the likeness of God has been created in righteousness and holiness of the truth."

James 4:7
"Submit therefore to God. Resist the devil and he will flee from you."

Colossians 3:10
"And have put on the new self who is being renewed to a true knowledge according to the image of the One who created him."

An important truth has been continually and purposely reiterated. The genuine Christian has become a new person, a new creature as defined in the Scripture. There has been a supernatural transformation within the core of our inner most being. It's imperative for the new born Christian to understand this fact. Neither religion nor reformation is the answer to man's pressing problem. The only remedy is transformation, and only Christ has the power to transform. Paul exhorts the believer to put off the old life; the old man who has plagued him, and in turn put on the new life, the new man who has been created in the image and likeness of Christ. As new creatures in Christ, we have been given a new mind. God's plan and purpose is to mold the Christian into the "image of His Son" (Romans 8:29). The struggle we face is with our unredeemed shell.

The new birth consists of a divine nature and the born-again believer is promised a new body in the future.

Until then, the Christian must contend with an unredeemed body. Each born again believer enters their new life in Christ with baggage from the past. As we have seen, alcohol and drug addiction will produce stinky thinking and poor behavior. This is all baggage from the past we must deal with. The old habits of a sinful past will seek to haunt and follow you. The temptation will be regression instead of progression. You must press forward as a new creature by resisting a mountain of old thought and behavior.

God miraculously delivered the Hebrews from Egyptian slavery and bondage. He then led them on a long journey through the wilderness toward the promise land. Their journey to this land of promise was not without difficulty. Their adventure led them through trying and difficult times, but God was continually with them. The addict will be confronted with many difficulties in his journey to recovery and should expect a struggle along the way. The Hebrew people were guilty of habitually complaining about their difficulties. They often failed to trust God who had delivered them from great toils in the past. During those difficult periods, many of them suggested it would have been better to remain in Egyptian slavery. The stinky thinking and baggage developed under Egyptian bondage followed them on their journey through the wilderness. Such thinking led them into unnecessary sufferings and difficulties. They needed to think with a different mindset. The way we think affects the way we behave and will determine the attitude we carry forward. They should have accepted the facts and concluded God was in complete control of every circumstance. God's people must believe He will see them through until the end, regardless of the situations they encounter. This is defined as walking by faith. Most are familiar with the biblical story regarding the resurrection of Lazarus from the dead.

So they removed the stone. Then Jesus raised His eyes, and said, "Father, I thank You that You have heard Me. I knew that you always hear me; but because of the people standing around I said it, so that they may believe that you sent me." When He had said these things, He cried out with a loud voice, "Lazarus, come forth." The man who had died came forth, bound hand and foot with wrappings, and his face was wrapped around with a cloth. Jesus said to them, "Unbind him, and let him go" (John 11:41-44).

Lazarus had been dead for three days when Jesus came upon the scene. He spoke life into a dead body and resurrected Lazarus from physical death. When Lazarus came out of the tomb, he was wearing the grave clothes which perhaps still reeked of death. He was bound by the wrappings of his burial cloth and would have had difficulty walking. In this story we see some possible insights into the spiritual resurrection or new birth. The born-again Christian is spiritually resurrected from the dead; however, he still experiences the stench of his old grave clothes. Like the grave clothes of Lazarus, old habits and stinky thinking do not automatically disappear with the new birth. It requires effort, diligence and perseverance to change one's dirty clothes and put on the new ones afforded by Christ. It often requires scrubbing to remove the dinginess that is ingrained in the unredeemed flesh. The process of practical sanctification or cleansing is not an overnight task, but the discipline of a lifetime requiring constant diligence and obedience.

There is an interesting story in the Book of Numbers aptly illustrating the stinky thinking of man in his sinful condition in (Numbers 13:2733).

Thus they told him, and said, "We went in to the land where you sent us; and it certainly does flow with milk and honey, and this is its fruit. Nevertheless, the people who live in the land are strong, and the cities are fortified and very large; and moreover, we saw the descendants of Anak there. Amalek is living in the land of the Negev and the Hittites and the Jebusites and the Amorites are living in the hill country, and the Canaanites are living by the sea and by the side of the Jordan." Then Caleb quieted the people before Moses and said, "We should by all means go up and take possession of it, for we will surely overcome it." But the men who had gone up with him said, "We are not able to go up against the people, for they are too strong for us." So they gave out to the sons of Israel a bad report of the land which they had spied out, saying, "the land, through which we have gone, in spying it out, is a land that devours its inhabitants; and all the people whom we saw in it are men of great size.

There also we saw the Nephilim (the sons of Anak are part of the Nephilim); and we became like grasshoppers in our own sight, and so we were in their sight."

The Hebrews had been delivered from Egypt and were approaching the promise land. In an effort to survey the situation they sent spies out to survey the land and determine their means of entrance. Twelve spies were sent out into the land. Upon returning with their report, the land was all God had promised and more, but all was not well with ten of those who were sent out. These ten spies chose to focus on obstacles rather than rest in the promises of God. As with the character of many addicts, they were pessimist instead of optimist and their stinky thinking was a hindrance to their sight. The result is they view the matter from a poor perspective. Their return displayed fear because they were enamored with the strength of those who inhabited the land, rather than trusting in the sovereign God who had rescued them miraculously from Egyptian slavery. Fear seized their minds, stinky thinking invaded their thought process, and they determined it could not be done. Fear overcame their faith and they succumbed to the enemy's suggestion. They were focusing on what were considered impossible odds. These individuals failed to remember who they were serving and following. The naysayers chose to overlook the power of a God who had miraculously delivered them from one danger after another throughout their wilderness journey. Rather than focus on the power of the Almighty, they drowned themselves in a sea of stinky thinking and returned in defeat. This is a mentality the new born child of God must contend with on his journey to experiencing victory. Stinky thinking is perhaps the greatest obstacle an addict will face in his journey toward sobriety and victorious living.

Twelve spies went out and returned. Ten came back permeated with fear because they focused on barriers, while two spies returned focused on the promises and faithfulness of God. They all agreed the land was everything and even more than God had promised. The two optimists did not deny there would be great obstacles to overcome. They simply chose to believe the same God who had brought them this far, would see them through as He had promised. The two faithful spies refused to indulge in stinky thinking, opting to believe God was far greater than anything standing in the way. They had begun to see and think with the eyes of faith. The optimists understood when God gave instruction to move forward and conquer; He would supply the power and means to accomplish the mission. God calls His people to clean, righteous, and holy living. He commands us to live right, rely upon Him, and trust Him by faith. God calls us to live a life of holiness and empowers us to live it. He never requires us to do the impossible.

Note again, they did not deny the existence of obstacles. They simply understood God was far greater and more powerful than all else. A faithful few considered and chose to believe that with God's help they would continue to conquer and move forward. It was simply a matter of choosing how they would view the situation and circumstance. Man may choose to remain being clothed with his dirty grave clothes, or he can determine with God's empowerment to put off the old grave clothes of stinky thinking, and dress himself up with the new man he has become in Christ. By faith the Christian can arise and face each new day with a victorious outlook. He can learn to think properly with a godly attitude by putting on the mind of Christ. Man must choose to set aside his old line of thinking. Poor thinking festers and hinders when allowed to mutate and hang around. The demolishment of stinky thinking is essential if the recovering addict is going to experience the reality of victory. God promised Israel the land; they were required to go out and subdue it with His help. God has given the recovering addict his freedom. He must go out and take it. The recovering addict must learn to be responsible and accountable for his own thinking.

The glass half-full of water serves as a great illustration of how man will choose to perceive any given issue. How someone sees a situation or circumstance is a matter of choice. He chooses to see the glass half empty and refuses to drink, or he sees the glass half full and makes the best use of what he has. Seeing the glass half empty is the essence of stinky thinking. Addicts are well known for their tendency to see the glass half empty; hence, they begin their new lives filled with a stinky thought process that must be dealt with and overcome. Ten of the spies said "we cannot," while two of them insisted they could.

This corrupted mindset must be set aside, removed and replaced with biblical thinking if the recovering addict is going to proceed toward victory over the obstacles at hand. Giving up becomes very easy when our thinking is marred by negative and dark thoughts. All obstacles cannot be avoided, but they can be overcome, and the Christian needs to accept this as fact. Life is filled with obstacles, trials and temptations which cannot always be avoided, but can be conquered. Paul covers this issue in his letter to the Corinthians.

No temptation has overtaken you but such as is common to man; and God is faithful, who will not allow you to be tempted beyond what you are able, but with the temptation will provide the way of escape also, so that you may be able to endure it (1 Corinthians 10:13).

God will never allow us to face more than we can endure and will not hinder us with obstacles beyond our capacity to conquer. He always provides a way of escape from the obstacles, temptations and trials that beset us. Another great illustration of choice regarding the thought process is discovered in the story of David and Goliath (1 Samuel 17:37).

And David said, "The LORD who delivered me from the paw of the lion and from the paw of the bear, He will deliver me from the hand of this Philistine." And Saul said to David, "Go, and may the LORD be with you."

The Army of Israel was in a stand down situation with the mighty giant Goliath and the Philistines. The challenge was killing Goliath, a giant of great statue and strength. Saul's army trembled in fear as the giant hurled great threatening words of insult and thundered with a fearsome threat of defiance. Israel's army failed to place their eyes on the God they served, choosing to focus on their fear of the mighty giant who ranted with great rage. They trembled at the thumping of his feet and waving of his arms. He taunted them with a voice of thunder and a tongue poisoned with disdain. Their minds were filled with stinky thinking as they observed this giant of a man. Fear flooded every fiber of their being as they faced what appeared to be an impossible situation. Good perception was an impossibility because they were viewing the predicament from their own stinky mindset rather than looking to God by faith. Many of these soldiers were trained men of war and mighty men of valor; yet they trembled in doubt when confronted with this giant problem. They focused on what was an impossible task in their own minds, rather than focus on the God who created and controls all things. They chose to see the glass half empty, rather than see it half full. In their minds they entertained the tremendous physique of the giant. As his threatening taunts resonated and grew, a defeated attitude took root in their minds which served to increase their fear of failure. All caught up in their stinky thought process they were paralyzed with fear and helplessness. As a result, they refused to move forward, confront the giant with faith, and conquer the mighty challenge standing before them.

Suddenly, on the scene arrives a little shepherd boy named David who had been sent to check on his brothers. He would become a mighty warrior and eventually prove himself as a great king of Israel. David was a man of faith. He had witnessed God bring down giants in his own life as a shepherd boy. Incensed at the threats of Goliath, he volunteered to challenge this giant Philistine and rid Israel of a rodent. David was a mere child in comparison to the mighty warriors who surrounded him in this battle. He considered not his own size, nor did he fear the statue of this mighty giant. David refused to view the glass as half empty! He chose to move on the assurance of faith, and understood the God of Israel was much greater than this giant of the Philistines. David thought with the mind of faith rather than choose a mind filled with doubt and stinky thought. The result was destruction of the giant with a sling shot that produced a great victory for Israel.

A mighty army filled with stinky thinkers was unable to do what one little shepherd boy was able to accomplish by putting his faith and trust in God. He faced what seemed to be impossible with the visible eye, and accomplished a mighty work through the invisible eye of faith. The power of faith can take us places where the naked eye would never dream or consider going. God specializes in leading His people through impossible situations when they are faithful to believe and act on faith. The mighty Army of Israel faced Goliath with the eyes of sight rather than the eyes of faith. Following after the ways of God will require spiritual growth and a determination to "walk by faith, not by sight" (2 Corinthians 5:7).

Addicts are often running from various giants in their lives. They tremble with overwhelming fear over issues too painful to deal with. The solution is to medicate their fears with alcohol or drugs. These barriers whether real or imagined come with seemingly impossible odds to overcome. Many of these giants are self-produced, while others are simply natural challenges we all face. In his stinky thinking, he believes he is an isolated case. The addict is notorious for running from his fears, rather than challenging, confronting, and dealing with them head on. The addict's stinky thinking has convinced him to focus on the impossibility of his situation, rather than accepting by faith the fortitude to move forward and conquer the giant taunting him. Recovering and recovered addicts are familiar with the Serenity Prayer. It contains a mountain of golden truth to be grasps and put into practice.

> "God grant me the serenity to accept the
> things I cannot change,
> the courage to change the things I can,
> and the wisdom to know the difference."

The Serenity Prayer promotes a key thinking process of making the transition from stinky grave clothes to proper thinking and agreement with God's word. Many addicts find themselves at a deadlock with issues in their lives of which they are simply incapable of changing. They foolishly dwell on issues they have no control over. The recovering addict must learn to accept certain realities, leave them in the past, and move forward. The great apostle Paul readily recognized he was unable to change his past and wrote, "Putting those things behind me, I press on toward the high calling of God in Christ Jesus" (Philippians 3:13).

It is pure foolishness to allow something you cannot change to prevent forward progress in life. Some issues you must simply accept and place behind you. These would be those matters of which you have no control over. Many addicts live in a time capsule stuck on issues they are incapable of changing. Insane thinking prevents them from moving forward. Undoubtedly, the past is filled with dirty laundry, dirty deeds, hurts, pains, and failures; however, those things cannot be changed. They must be released, let go, and left in the past! Get on your face before the sovereign God who is in control; confess your failures, hurts, sins, mistakes, and the pains of your past. This is nothing unique; we all have issues of the past. Ask God to forgive your past sins, cleanse you of them, and choose to leave them there with Him. Perhaps you need to deal with an individual from the past and make things right. Put forth your best effort to heal broken relationships, move forward and leave the past behind. Once you understand God has forgiven you, step up and forgive yourself. "If we confess our sins, He is faithful and righteous to forgive us our sins and to cleanse us from all unrighteousness" (1 John 1:9). Forgiving ourselves as God forgives us is a necessary part in letting go of the past. God has forgiven you! Accept it, forgive yourself and move on.

Some things you are capable of changing. With God's help, such change is not only possible, but inevitable when you persevere in the faith. A change of situation and circumstance may not happen immediately; perhaps it will take some time to work through. With God's help, self is the only individual anyone will ever change. Changing others is not one of those issues we have the capability or power to implement. We cannot make someone else love us, accept us, approve of us, or like us. Our focus must be on changing issues and matters with self.

The greatest focus should be changing the way we think. This is by far the greatest challenge of transitioning from the old way of life into the new. Poor reasoning has become a habitual habit for many, and old habits can be difficult to break. The recovering addict must learn to view everything from an absolute, eternal, and biblical perspective. The absolute and eternal facts of life are found in the written word of God. His word must be the recovering addict's manual for life. What's the one thing in life bothering you the most? What is the one thing you would change about self if you had the power to proceed? If you can change it, get busy, move forward and deal with it. If you are incapable of changing it, let it go, and move forward. What's the one thing you would change about someone else if you possessed the power? Forget it, you don't have the power! Why waste time on something you do not have the ability or capability of accomplishing?

The solutions to all of life's problems can be found in the word of God. The Alcoholic and Narcotic Anonymous books are not sufficient sources of truth for overcoming bondage to sin. They simply do not have the facts, nor do they agree with the word of God in some areas. Only the word of God contains the absolutes of life and the power to change a man's way of thinking. The recovering addict must bathe and saturate his mind with the truth. The word of God has the power to change your way of thinking; it also contains the wisdom to teach you how to discern between the things you can change and those things you cannot. It will provide you with the needed wisdom to live in a world filled with chaos and darkness. How futile for an addict or anyone else to fret, worry, and focus on things that cannot be changed. How foolish to spend a lifetime centering on matters of impossibility. Focus on those things you are capable of changing. Many people spend a lifetime punishing and destroying self for something they have no control over. You must focus your energies and efforts on changing the things you have the power to change. Leave everything else to God who is fully capable of dealing with those issues. Conquering the challenges of these control issues will greatly enhance your progress toward the ultimate victory of recovery.

The primary means of setting aside the old man and shedding the old grave clothes is to diligently study God's word, pray and spend time with others who have a sound personal relationship with Christ. Moving beyond the bondage of addiction, you will discover great amounts of time and space to fill. You should occupy it with productive efforts and activities. The time once spent drinking and abusing drugs should be spent on producing and maintaining a sober lifestyle. Church attendance will be a very important element of your recovery and spiritual growth process. Finding a scriptural based recovery program would be beneficial; although, such programs may be difficult to locate, depending upon your location. No one understands a recovering addict as well as another; "it takes one to know one." Unless a person has been there, it's beyond their capacity to fully understand the mental, emotional and spiritual consequences of addiction. Sound biblical addiction recovery programs are difficult to locate; however, they do exist, and can be found via internet searches. Among some of those are Alcoholic's Victorious, Reformer's Unanimous, and Celebrate Recovery. These programs may or may not be available in your area. A truly effective recovery program should be strictly based on Scripture rather than a worldly philosophy. Be careful and weary of Twelve Step programs expressing worldly solutions. Unfortunately, this can be the case with some church sponsored programs that think like the world. The foundation of a successful recovery plan must be founded on the word of God, and promote Jesus Christ as the only Higher Power.

Jesus told the story of an individual who was delivered of an evil spirit. Eventually the spirit would return to check out the home he had previously left. Upon the spirits return he found the house empty and called in more spirits to take up residence.

> Now when the unclean spirit goes out of a man, it passes through waterless places seeking rest, and does not find it. Then it says, "I will return to my house from which I came;" and when it comes, it finds it unoccupied, swept, and put in order. Then it goes and takes along with it seven other spirits more wicked than itself, and they go in and live there; and the last state of that man becomes worse than the first (Matthew 12:43-45).

Even some secular programs suggest that each time a person returns to alcohol or drug use after an extended period of abstinence, the addict's condition perhaps increases to the extent as if he had not ever abstained, and he is worse off than previously. When the addict ceases using his substance of choice, there will be a void that must be filled with something. The addict's life, time, and space have been consumed by his addictive lifestyle. Change requires a filling of this void left within from the absence of addictive behavior. Many mistakenly become obsessed with recovery programs and take them to the extreme in an attempt to replace the void. While active participation in programs and groups may be necessary, a recovering addict must be careful and not allow a program to take the place of God. The void of time and space can be filled with many things. Jesus Christ alone can saturate the void, satisfy the spiritual hunger, and quench the thirst of a human soul in need. The recovering addict must fill the space once saturated by alcohol and drugs with the word of God, the kingdom of God, His righteousness, and the will of God. Make the word of God your Big Book!

Spend all the time you desire devouring its pages to discover the issues of life and how to deal with them. God's word is a cleansing agent, and will work the supernatural element of sanctification within your new born spirit. It's powerful, and will produce the necessary change within to move forward toward progress in God's perfect will. It would be a great investment to place the time you once spent drinking and drugging into the word of God. The Scriptures are filling and satisfying to the new man; however, they will be repulsive to the unredeemed flesh. The word of God is a powerful tool, extremely capable and proficient in fulfilling its purpose. The time and effort you once put into the old sinful self should be invested in spiritual maturation and development of the new person you have become in Christ. Years spent creating a total wreck will not be made up overnight. The new person you have become desires and longs for the things of God. Spend your time wisely by feeding the spiritual man and starving the old man.

The new man must feed on the truth. The new creature in Christ desires to grow in righteousness and holiness. You must focus on setting the old man aside and persist in clothing the new man with the things of God. Old habits and ways will be set aside as you learn to walk in newness of life. God's Addiction Recovery Plan and The Biblical Path to Freedom lead the addict to this fact: **I must set aside the old life and put on the new life I have been given in Jesus Christ.**

Chapter 10
Separating From Threats

Freedom Step Nine

I must separate myself from people and places threatening to lure me back into the old lifestyle.

2 Corinthians 6:17
"Therefore, come out from their midst and be separate, says the Lord."

Psalm 1:1
"How blessed is the man who does not walk in the counsel of the wicked, nor stand in the path of sinners, nor sit in the seat of scoffers."

1 Peter 1:15
"But like the Holy One who called you, be holy yourselves also in all your behavior; because it is written, you shall be holy, for I am holy."

Beginning a new way of life presents some unique challenges and requires the recovering addict to make some difficult choices from the very onset of his recovery journey. This new way of living will demand separation from detrimental people, places, and things of the past. This can prove to be a troubling and difficult challenge. The refusal to separate self from certain threats is a contributing factor to many slips, failures, and relapses. An addict's life has been built around the world of addiction. He is shrouded in a cesspool of poor choices, dark places and contagious relationships. People generally surround themselves with others of like character and habit. Often, the addict's behavior and character have driven away most, if not all healthy relationships.

The old saying "birds of a feather flock together" is certainly true of the addict. Another very applicable adage is, "it takes one to know one." Place an addict in a new environment and it will not take him very long to discover where to locate his medicine. He will quickly find another addict who can lead him to the source of his desired drug of choice. This is why the geographical cure is seldom effective.   This is a mythical remedy suggesting that simply moving to another location will solve the addict's problem. A change of location is never an effective means of escaping addiction. It's simply another mode of the stinky thinking syndrome and a means of denial. It's another excuse suggesting the real problem is environment. The addict seems to instinctively know and attract his own kind. The lifestyle of an addict dictates who his friends will be, as well as where he may be found at certain times.

Addicts are well known for destroying healthy relationships while building a pyramid of unhealthy ones. The addict and the sober person live in two separate worlds, many miles apart, and are divided by a great gulf of practical reasoning. This is why sober people have such great difficulty in understanding an addictive lifestyle. Freedom step nine brings a recovering addict to the place of having to make some very difficult choices. The sobriety and freedom available in following Christ must be maintained at all costs. Nothing can be allowed to stand in the way. Unhealthy relationships must be set aside in order to develop healthier ones. The recovering addict must establish new friends who will encourage and assist him in his journey toward recovery. He must learn quickly; anything or anyone threatening his new life of sobriety must be set aside, separated from, and forsaken. His life and recovery depend upon it. This is another one of the recovering addict's great challenges that is not an option in God's Addiction Recovery Plan. The Biblical Path to Freedom calls for a life of separation. There must be a detachment from everything and everyone standing in the way of recovery.

Visiting the same old hangouts and loitering with the same old crowd is a recipe for disaster. A recovering alcoholic will never survive sitting on a barstool and attempting to drink soda, while fellowshipping with others who are imbibing in alcohol and drug use. A recovering cocaine addict will never survive hanging around others who are snorting lines or hitting the crack pipe. The old places and friends must be completely forsaken if the addict is to discover success on his journey toward recovery. New friends and new places must be sought out and put into place.

The greatest means of beginning the new life is finding a good solid biblical based church and becoming a part of the family. Once you have found a good church, sit down with the pastor and let him know of your decision for Christ. Be upfront and honest about the challenges you are facing. Nothing can substitute for good godly counsel; you're going to need help from the knowledge and wisdom of others. Be in church each time the door is open. This will serve to fill the excess time on your hands as a result of abstinence. Don't expect to feel comfortable and at home when you first enter the door of any church. Get involved and be fanatically committed to Sunday school, regular worship, Bible studies, and whatever groups may be available at your church of choice. A later chapter will provide good information on how to find and become part of a good church home. You must fill the void of time with healthy activities and friends.

The salvation you have freely received in Christ can never be lost. You now have an eternal home in heaven with Christ, provided you have truly accepted Him as Lord and Savior. Jesus promised abundant life to those who would follow Him (John 10:10). The abundance of life you experience in the future will be determined by the good or bad choices you make in the present. The Scripture tells us, "For whatever a man sows, this he will also reap" (Galatians 6:7). If you are to enjoy life in its fullest as God intends, you must make choices in accordance with the word of God. There are always consequences to our actions. Making wrong choices creates negative consequences, while good choices create positive consequences. Every addict on the street has arrived at his destination due to poor choices. At some time in his past, he made a conscious decision to take his first drink, pop the first pill, snort that first line, hit the first rock or run up his first fix. From that point forward, a chain of events followed and led the addict to a dead- end street. This is the very reason why churches and pastors should be dogmatic on the subject of abstinence from alcohol and illegal drug use. Those who never take the first drink, or use a drug, will never end up an addict on the street.

The very moment you became a child of God, you became an enemy of a dark spiritual realm and entered into a raging battle. God often uses and speaks to us through other people. Likewise, the enemy will use and speak through others in an attempt to lead us astray and rob us of the abundant life God has promised. The addict remaining in the lifestyle you are leaving behind, must be rejected and set aside. He is a dangerous and deceptive threat to your sobriety! Maintaining old relationships and visiting those old places of ill repute will only serve as disruptive stumbling blocks. They cannot serve any positive enforcement on your new adventure. Those old places you once visited must be forsaken and avoided! You may need to find a new route to and from work. You may need to travel an extra mile or two in bypassing the establishment you once frequently visited. There must be avoidance at all costs. In the beginning, your weakness makes you vulnerable and susceptible to every alluring threat.

At the onset of recovery, it will be important to avoid as many triggers as possible. Triggers are those people, places and things that will seek to draw your mind back into the past. They can quickly serve as temptations to make the wrong choice. These are akin to the old man, the old system and means that brought the addict to his bottom. They must die and be set aside with the old man and the filthy grave clothes. Setting them aside will assist you in putting on the new man. There is no other way to move forward. In order to make progress, you must set aside all people, places and relationships that would threaten to lead you back into a pit of sin and addiction.

It becomes essential to surround yourself with others who are not filled with the stinky thought syndrome. When you subject yourself to the stinky thinking and reasoning of others, you're opening up your mind to the old trains of thought. You're pulling the trigger of your own mind by placing yourself in stinky surroundings. If you're attempting to quit smoking, the worst thing you can do is stand beside someone lighting up. The smell of smoke will immediately trigger the brain with an urge to participate. This has been true of people who have quit for twenty or thirty years. The brain is filled with memory and trigger points. Straight people will help you see and understand poor thinking habits. The mind of the addict coming out of addiction is immersed in a thick fog that hinders his ability to see and think clearly. These old friends and places will only serve as land mines filled with stinky thoughts to drag you back into negative thought patterns. The apostle Paul wrote, "Do not be deceived: bad company corrupts good morals" (1 Corinthians 15:33). Like gang members, addicts have their own language, symbols, and unique ways of living and communicating. Their lives are controlled by dark forces seeking to do them and others harm. It's imperative for you to surround yourself with others who have learned to think properly, those who can recognize and correct your old patterns of thinking as they surface. Find a new crowd familiar with the ways and thoughts of God. Seek out a wise group who will support you in striving to maintain a life of sobriety free from drugs and alcohol, or whatever your downfall may be. You're going to need some dependable friends who will truly love you in your quest for victory.

Consider the classic movie Cool Hand Luke. Paul Newman played the role of a prisoner named Luke. He was being held in a work camp, serving on a chain gang for criminals. Luke's major problem was in getting his mind to think right. He was a criminal who had saturated his mind with stinky thinking. He was a wise guy. Boss Man did all he could to change Luke's rebellious and stubborn way of thinking. Luke's responsibility in prison was to abide by the rules and do as Boss Man directed him, but he refused and rejected the idea of getting his mind right. He abhorred the idea of cleansing his mind of poor thinking habits. He was a master of manipulation and gamesmanship. He surrounded himself with others of like character who thought as he did. Luke's choice of maintaining his own way of thinking eventually led to his death. The recovering addict must choose and be determined to change his way of thinking. Changing your way of thinking is impossible when you keep company with those who think like addicts. It's a futile effort to seek change while at the same time hanging around in the same old places, listening to the same old crowd, watching the same old movies and listening to the same old jokes. Someone has defined insanity as "continuing to do the same old thing and expecting a different result." Herein is found another one of the addict's greatest obstacles. Doing the same old thing only serves to produce a continued cycle of insanity. When an addict continues in this cycle of insanity, the same old results are produced over and over again. He lives on a merry-go-round, ever circling in an endless cycle of failure, despair and futility.

Freedom step nine has proven to be vital to any addict's recovery. Old friends will show up as the enemy seeks to use them as a tool of discovering just how serious the addict is about recovery. When a person comes to Jesus Christ, he must be willing to forsake all and follow Him, whatever the costs.

Jesus shared the story about a merchant in search of a costly pearl. Notice what the merchant did upon finding this pearl and understanding the value of what he had discovered. He determined to give up everything else for this precious pearl. The pearl of a sober life is found in Jesus Christ. "Again, the kingdom of heaven is like a merchant seeking fine pearls, and upon finding one pearl of great value, he went and sold all that he had and bought it" (Matthew 13:45-46).

Here is the essence of giving up the past and thrusting all you have into newness of life. The addict must separate from the old ways; he must cut his ties from those elements of the past which will only serve to drag him back into despair and anguish. Making the determination to separate from the old lifestyle, the old ways, and the same old crowd, will help the addict move forward with his new life in Christ, and serve to strengthen his resolve. Sobriety is much more than abstaining from alcohol and drug usage; it's a complete lifestyle change affecting every aspect of the recovering addict's existence. He must separate himself from those people, places and things serving to promote a continued cycle of failure. The recovering addict must be willing to forsake all in his quest for sobriety.

Jesus illustrates the urgency of leaving everything else behind when we determine to follow Him. The story is of three individuals who initially claimed they were willing to follow Him. Problems arose when they insisted on procrastinating and taking care of other business before starting the journey.

> As they were going along the road, someone said to Him, "I will follow you wherever You go." And Jesus said to him, "The foxes have holes and the birds of the air have nests, but the Son of Man has nowhere to lay His head." And He said to another, "Follow Me." But he said, "Lord, permit me first to go and bury my father." But He said to him, "Allow the dead to bury their own dead; but as for you, go and proclaim everywhere the kingdom of God." Another also said, "I will follow You, Lord; but first permit me to say good-bye to those at home." But Jesus said to him, "No one, after putting his hand to the plow and looking back, is fit for the kingdom of God" (Luke 9:57-62).

Addicts are well known for their propensity and tendency to procrastinate. Putting things off until tomorrow is not a biblically acceptable principle. Procrastination is putting off until tomorrow what should be done today. God calls us to move forward and progress in His call upon our lives. Tomorrow may be too late! The addict must be willing to put the past behind and move ahead today. This quest must begin immediately! I'll quit later, or I'll go tomorrow is never an acceptable attitude. The old friends, old places, and even family must be set aside if necessary.

> Jesus said, "He who loves father or mother more than Me is not worthy of Me; and he who loves son or daughter more than Me is not worthy of Me. And he who does not take his cross and follow after Me is not worthy of Me" (Matthew 10:37-38).

The addict desiring freedom must break loose from anything threatening to lure him back. He must separate himself from all stumbling blocks. God's Addiction Recovery Plan and The Biblical Path to Freedom lead the addict to this fact: **I must separate myself from people and places threatening to lure me back into the old lifestyle.**

Chapter 11

Sharing The Good News

Freedom Step Ten

I must share my new life with others, and lead them toward the knowledge of Christ.

Matthew 28:19-20
"Go therefore and make disciples of all the nations, baptizing them in the name of the Father, and the Son, and the Holy Spirit, teaching them to observe all that I have commanded you and I am with you always, even to the end of the age.

Mark 5:19
"Go home to your people and report to them what great things the Lord has done for you, and how He had mercy on you."

Acts 1:8
"But you will receive power when the Holy Spirit has come upon you; and you shall be My witnesses."

Sharing and reaching out to others is an integral part of any successful recovery program. You have been set free from spiritual death, given a new life, delivered from darkness and bondage to sin. There should be a desire to share the hope you have discovered with others who are seeking freedom from addiction. The recovered addict found freedom because someone else cared enough to reach out and share the availability of hope. Your continued recovery requires you to reach out with love and concern toward others. This will be one of the primary purposes of your new-found life in Christ. Ministry to others will assist you in continuing to fill the void.

The initial attitude of a recovering addict and new Christian often becomes a burning desire to help everyone, to launch out and save the world from self-destruction. The recovered or recovering addict will eventually face an inevitable realization, not everyone wants your help. You cannot save someone determined and intent to go their own way. Every addict cannot be convinced to see things your way; however, you can tell them of your new-found freedom and share with them the joy of being sober. You can make yourself available. When they are ready to seek peace, joy, righteousness, and freedom from bondage, they will look to you. They will understand you have been there and can relate. Be prepared for a lifetime of rejection when reaching out to others. The most rewarding of all your endeavors will be the one you are instrumental in helping. Jesus reached out to thousands during His three years of ministry, while only a few received and accepted the fullness of His offer. The joy of reaching just one will be well worth the effort. God desires to use you, your knowledge, wisdom and experience in reaching out to others with the goal of leading them toward forgiveness of sin and freedom from addiction.

Dependency on substances creates progressive misery, mental anguish, physical ailments and pain. Many miss the fact that pain is an instrumental tool in bringing the addict to his bottom or point of realization. One of the cruelest things an individual can do for an addict is bail him out of the pain and suffering caused by his addiction. The addict chooses to live as he does, and should be allowed to suffer the consequences of his actions. To assist him in maintaining his addiction is to play the role of an enabler. An enabler is someone who helps the addict escape from accountability and responsibility for his own actions. Enabler's are often guilty of playing God, and fails to understand the Creator established pain as a means of alerting us of a problem. Pain is an instrumental tool in bringing an addict to his senses. When someone dares to play God and relieve the pain without addressing the problem, they are aiding and abetting the addict in his addiction. They are actually contributing to his slow suicidal death, rather than leading him to resolve his problem. To enable someone in their drug or alcohol abuse is to aid and abet them in their own destruction. Many addicts have enabler's who are guilty of preventing them from realizing they need help. If an addict can rely on an enabler to pay his rent or his electric bill, he has no reason to be responsible himself. Do not be found guilty of holding an addict back from proceeding toward his bottom.

Never aid and abet the addict in his addiction by contributing to his ability to maintain his habit.

Some addicts reach bottom more quickly than others while many find a bottom. The end for some will be insanity or death. All addicts are at different places and stages along the road to destruction. Those who are beginning their journey will prove to be the most difficult to reach. The addict starting out on his march down this destructive path has no idea where he is, nor does he foresee the consequences he will ultimately experience. He is more interested in having a good time, living in a fantasy land and feeling euphoric. It's a mentality of living for today, oblivious and unaware of the price to be paid tomorrow. He cannot see beyond his present status and grasp a glimpse of the misery ahead. The addict is certain he can handle it. He is convinced his current enjoyment will never become a problem for him personally. With blinded eyes and deaf ears, he fails to see and hear the danger approaching. He is a blind maniac running wide open toward a cliff, unaware of the heartache, chaos and torment awaiting ahead.

Those nearing or having reached bottom will be the easiest to reach. The painful consequences of their actions over the years have taken a great toll. The addict having begun the experience of losing precious relationships and other cherished elements of life, will have the capacity to see his problem becoming worse, as sin progresses along its treacherous path. Addiction is like a progressive cancer devouring the heart, soul, and mind of its victim. In this sense addiction can be described as a destructive disease. The addict having lost everything has nothing left to lose and is most often fruitful ground for ministry. He may listen with an open ear and receive the seeds of hope offered. Here is a prime prospect for reaching out with the message of recovery, salvation, and freedom from bondage to sin. It may be days, weeks, months, or years before the seeds take root and produce fruit. You've been there and have common ground. You can relate and become a voice of hope in the dark world of addiction.

Recovery can appear to be instantaneous and miraculous. It can also be a long drawn out journey requiring great patience on the part of those trying to help. Those who require the greatest amount of time in the recovery process will need the continued attention and care of others who have gone before them. It requires painstaking patience, discernment, and tough love at times. Many long-term addicts have caused brain damage and harm to other organs of their body. The mental anguish and emotional stress on the body will sometimes require years of hard work and effort. The recovering addict will find help in others who have gone before them on the road to recovery. The recovered will be an encourager, an example, a source of hope and promise. The recovered and recovering addict will be able to relate and confirm their similar experiences with others.

A story in the fifth chapter of Mark's gospel is a great portrayal of this important step. Jesus miraculously brought about the deliverance of a man who had been possessed by demons (Mark 5:1-20). This poor demonic bound man lived a pitiful and tormented life. His home was the graveyard; he lived among the dead. His life consisted of ranting and raving in the darkness throughout the night. He had lost his mind and was out of control. The man was a total wreck who had already gone off the cliff and was well beyond the help of normal assistance. People had attempted to help him in the past. Perhaps he had been given up as a homeless and a hopeless case. He was like the addict who has seen one recovery program after another to no avail. No one was able to help him break free from the captivity of his soul. He was a suicidal maniac, a raving lunatic, a madman who had totally lost his mind. This man was enslaved and living in complete bondage to Satan as his master. He had been robbed of all sanity and self-respect. Here is a great story lending hope to the fact that no one is beyond the possibility of deliverance and recovery. Society often gives up on the addict and writes him off as hopeless. What appears impossible to man, is possible with a God who specializes in accomplishing things man is incapable of doing for self or others. Jesus Christ is able to change the most vile and hideous creature into something lovely and beautiful. He has done it over and over again throughout history.

Jesus met this demon possessed man at his point and place of need. Those who would be instrumental in helping others must follow the attitude of Jesus in ministry. He spoke deliverance and recovery to a lost man who had spent his days wandering among the darkness and the dead. With the words of His mouth and the authority of His divine power, Jesus Christ set this man free from the evils of enslavement. The story continues and discloses to us his new condition when all was said and done. People of the region "came to Jesus and observed the man who had been demon possessed, sitting down, clothed, and in his right mind" (Mark 5:15). As a result of this miraculous deliverance, the man fell in love with Jesus and sought to remain by His side.

> As He was getting into the boat, the man who had been demon-possessed was imploring Him that he might accompany Him. And He did not let him, but He said to him, "Go home to your people and report to them what great things the Lord has done for you, and how He had mercy on you." And he went away and began to proclaim in Decapolis what great things Jesus had done for him; and everyone was amazed (Mark 5:18-20).

In his right mind, he is now capable of living a normal life among others. Leaving this land of death, he is free to testify of a miraculous deliverance God had wrought in his life. This man resided in the graveyard with a habit of streaking through it naked. He practiced cutting himself and screamed throughout late hours of the night. When does the alcoholic and drug addict face his most difficult battles? Suffering comes in the late hours, in the darkness of seclusion and reclusion. Now he is free and in his right mind. The freed demoniac received a new lease on life. He met someone able and willing to satisfy the deepest need of his troubled soul. Peace flooded his heart, joy filled his soul, and sanity returned to his mind. The story moves forward telling of the man's strong desire to follow and be with Jesus wherever He went. This is a common and appropriate attitude of those whom God delivers out of great darkness and bondage.

There is a great burden of guilt lifted when a mountain of sin is forgiven. The result is a grateful heart seeking to please God in all things.
Jesus explains this relief in speaking of a woman who experienced much forgiveness. "For this reason, I say to you, her sins, which are many, have been forgiven, for she loved much; but he who is forgiven little, loves little" (Luke 7:47). It's a glorious moment when the recovering addict begins to see and hear what truth has done for him, when he begins to experience the beauty of living

free from the bondage that once plagued his soul. Truth suddenly becomes a quest of the heart, and it fervently seeks after God. Such an understanding is to realize what the Psalmist learned about life. "As the deer pants for the water brooks, so my soul pants for You, O God" (Psalm 42:1). Knowing and being with Jesus becomes the focal point of one's life when true freedom is experienced. Jesus would not allow this man to physically follow Him that day. He gave the man instruction as to what his mission would be. From this day forward, he would go out and share his deliverance with others. God expects no less of those who have experienced being set free from the awful throws of addiction.

Although Jesus did not allow this man to literally follow Him, He gave the man precise instruction as to his mission. He was to go home and tell his friends. In this sense, the man was allowed to follow both the Person and the command of Jesus. The same command is for all who would truly follow Jesus Christ. The call is for each of us to share with others what God has done for us. The recovering addict who has been set free by Jesus Christ has a unique story to tell regarding his own deliverance and recovery. It's a story of God's grace, mercy, forgiveness, love, redemption, salvation and deliverance. A testimony of a new-found freedom from the chains and shackles which once tied our hands and feet. Here is a message of hope for millions of others who are bound by the balls and chains of addiction.

Reaching out and helping others with issues and problems will be an important practice in the recovery process. Sharing is a major part of God's Addiction Recovery Plan. Striving to share and help others in need will be the agenda of your future journey and adventure with Christ. God's desire is for you to share with others what He has done for you. He will bring others across your path and present you with the opportunity to empathize with their hurts, thoughts, needs, fears, burdens and concerns. You will be blessed with a compassionate, merciful, patient, understanding and burdened heart, destined to reach out toward those experiencing the same pains and woes that once entangled you.

You will often face rejection in your outreach to others. Jesus was no stranger to negative reactions. He ministered to thousands who rejected His offer of salvation. Some are simply not interested in any truth you have to share, and saving every addict is an impossible task.

Perhaps you have heard the story of the young lad and the multitude of Starfish he discovered on the seashore one day? Starfish covered the beach, and the young boy would reach down to cast one at a time back into the sea. An older gentleman passing by noticed the boy's unceasing effort to return the Starfish back to their proper place in the ocean. He spoke to the young lad saying, "Son, you cannot save all of these Starfish, what does it matter." The young boy in turn stooped down, tossed another back into the sea and replied "it matters to that one."

Resist the urge to become disillusioned and discouraged by others. It will become a means of suffering with Christ. The heart of God aches for those living in slavery to addiction. This will be a unique cross you have been called to carry. Some are not interested in your help. Many will not be receptive to your attempts of outreach. Until they reach their own bottom and are ready for help, you can only make yourself available. The addict not ready for help will be one of those aspects of the serenity prayer you must remember; "Lord, help me to accept the things I cannot change." You can pray and cry out to the One who is able to change their hearts and open up their blinded eyes, but you are incapable of changing or forcing them to change and accept the truth.

The new born Christian has the capacity and ability to experience life the way God intended. You will find yourself progressively becoming an instrumental tool in the hand of a loving and merciful God. His desire is to use you in leading others away from the death, darkness, misery, and woe reaped as a result of their sin and rebellion. He will call on you to point others toward His plan of redemption. Someone loved and reached out to you in your addictive struggles. God now calls on you to reach out to others who are struggling and in desperate need of hope. God's Addiction Recovery Plan and The Biblical Path to Freedom lead the addict to this fact: **I must share my new life with others, and lead them toward the knowledge of Christ.**

Chapter 12
The Struggling Christian

How do children learn to walk? A child must be persistent and determined to rise with each stumble until balance and steadiness are perfected. Rarely, if ever will they succeed in their first attempt to walk. It's a reasonable assumption that walking comes easier for some than others. If a child were to simply give up after his first few attempts, he would never walk. Eventually the child gets it right and moves forward toward further maturity in physical growth and development. One of the child's future challenges will be learning to ride a bicycle. In all likelihood a couple of scrapes and bruises will be acquired in his attempt to stay on two wheels. How will the child ever learn to ride a bike? By getting up and continuing his quest to learn and perfect his balance. God has the prerogative of delivering an addict in a miraculous fashion should He choose. On the other hand, God most often allows a struggle in the process. This will generally be the scenario when an addict begins his quest for victory. Struggle is an essential means of the learning process in spiritual growth and development. There will be struggles in breaking free from longtime habitual behaviors and maintaining sobriety. Victory is experienced in persevering through the battles.

Psychological and physiological addiction will linger with the initial separation from alcohol and drugs. The mind as well as the body must be cleansed of impurities. Recovery is an enduring process requiring time. You must make up your mind to acquire and maintain a course of sobriety. Here is another great key to victory. Make up your mind and be determined to accept the blessings and talents God has given you. Victory is yours! Persevere with the tenacious determination of a Pit Bull, and you will come to experience victorious living in Christ. Through the ensuing struggle, God will grow, strengthen, teach, and instill within the needed wisdom, knowledge and power to sustain you. This process will prove to develop godly character and strong faith. Such faith will serve to conquer future mountains and obstacles. God uses battles to build character, produce stamina, and grow faith. No one ever fails until they give up. I heard a preacher once proclaim, "I'll quit when God fails." God will never fail! Put your faith, trust, and confidence in Him; for He does not have the capacity to fail. Be aware of and accept this precious promise: God "is able to do far more abundantly beyond all that we ask or think, according to the power that works in us" (Ephesians 3:20). Believe the word of God given to us through the prophet Jeremiah.

> Ah Lord God, Behold, you have made the heavens and the earth by your great power and by your outstretched arm! Nothing is too difficult for you. "Behold, I am the Lord, the God of all flesh; is anything too difficult for Me" (Jeremiah 32:17, 27).

A genuine Christian may falter and experience setbacks in his quest for freedom from fleshly hooks. Perseverance is of the utmost necessity in the determination to break loose. Be quick to acknowledge and confess your sins to God. Be steadfast with persistent prayer in your battle to break free. Never giving up is key to victory! Remember, God has given you the victory in Christ; the chains have already been broken. His spiritual power residing within will bring you through. How much time will victory in this struggle require? No one can say with certainty, but it will come. The combined power of a divine nature and the Holy Spirit will eventually prevail. The victory will come! Hold on to the altar of promise until sunshine arrives. The Psalmist wrote, "His favor is for a lifetime; weeping may last for the night, but a shout of joy comes in the morning" (Psalm 30:5). Someone has said, "The darkest hour is just before the dawn." The morning light will eventually bring forth a glorious victory. God never promises this Christian pilgrimage will be without struggle. Quite to the contrary, Jesus made the promise that trouble would come to those who follow Him. "These things I have spoken to you, so that in Me you may have peace. In the world you have tribulation, but take courage; I have overcome the world" (John 16:33).

God has promised to see His people through whatever we may face. He will provide the strength to endure, persevere, and gain victory over troubling times. The determined Christian will discover and experience the same truth

Paul received as God's word gripped his heart. "My grace is sufficient" (2 Corinthians 12:9). His grace is more than sufficient to manage the struggles we are confronted with. Another great promise of God is found in Paul's letter to the Romans. "The Law came in so that the transgression would increase; but where sin increased, grace abounded all the more" (Romans 5:20).

The Christian is not beyond sinning and becoming addicted to a substance. Whatever we yield ourselves to will have an impact upon our lives. Open up the door and the devil will be quick to step through it. Drug and alcohol abuse will lead anyone to physical and psychological addiction. The child of God daring to habitually participate in active disobedience against God's desires will be torn between two opposing powers. Drugs and alcohol can have the same effect upon a Christian as it does on an individual who has no knowledge of Christ. The good news is deliverance and victory is available to the Christian, as well as the lost sinner. The professing Christian struggling with addiction should first follow Paul's exhortation to the Corinthians. "Test yourselves to see if you are in the faith; examine yourselves" (2 Corinthians 13:5). Professing Christ and knowing Christ are two different issues. Jesus gave a stern warning that should be contemplated by us all.

> Not everyone who says to Me, Lord, Lord, will enter the kingdom of heaven, but he who does the will of My Father who is in heaven will enter. Many will say to Me on that day, "Lord, Lord, did we not prophesy in Your name, and in Your name cast out demons, and in Your name perform many miracles?" And then I will declare to them, "I never knew you; depart from Me, you who practice lawlessness" (Matthew 7:21-23).

There is a sad reality haunting genuine Christianity today. Everyone professing to be a Christian is not necessarily a born-again believer. Religion tends to assure people they are someone other than who they actually are. Satan uses religion to convince men they are right with God, while all along leading them down a destructive path of deception. There are many voices in the realm of professing Christianity preaching what Paul defined as "a different gospel" (Galatians 1:6). He warns of those who "want to distort the gospel of Christ" (Galatians 1:7). A distorted gospel will twist the truth in order to deceive its victims. A good percentage of those professing to be Christians have never really been born again. They have been deceived by religion and are unfamiliar with the genuine Christ of Scripture. Religion has a plethora of faces and many have been deceived by distorted gospels. They are but mere religions having no power to save and miraculously transform the inner spirit. "Holding to a form of godliness, although they have denied its power" (2 Timothy 3:5).

Religion is man's attempt by his own works to bring himself into a right relationship with God. It seeks to reform man and make him acceptable via his own righteousness. Biblical Christianity is an internal transforming experience and has nothing to do with outward show. The new birth is a miraculous act of transformation by the Spirit of God who imputes Christ's righteousness and makes a man right with God. Man cannot deliver himself from sin; nor can he save himself by doing good things. Man is utterly incapable of making the necessary change within his inner person required to become right with God. No amount of reformation, religion or good works will secure a personal relationship with God. A great illustration of this issue is the life and nature of a hog.

A hog's primary domain is his sty, and he possesses the nature that he was born with. He is destined to eat slop, wallow in filth, and cherishes the smell of his home. You can take a hog out of his natural environment, give him a bath, scrub him thoroughly, paint his toenails, make him smell sweet, and place a pretty pink ribbon around his neck. Upon completion, you have made the hog clean and pretty on the outside. You may have taken him out of his natural habitat, built him a clean structure, or even take him into your own home. Regardless of how much you primp him, he remains a hog. He has been externally reformed, but there has been no internal change. If you place him back in his natural habitat, he will resort to his old ways and reveal his hoggish nature. Herein the danger and deception of mere religion is exposed. You can take the hog out of the sty, but you can't take the sty out of the hog.

The same is true of the natural born sinner. Religion can clean a sinner up on the outside and make him look real pretty to the naked eye. On the inside he remains a sinner with no internal change. Reformation is not an adequate means or acceptable path of righteousness with God. There must be a

supernatural change within, transforming the sinner into a justified, cleansed, and sanctified child of God. This is the only means of becoming acceptable by God's standard. A natural sinner has no righteous standing with God, regardless of how good he may appear externally. The Pharisees were the most religious people of the day when Jesus arrived on the scene of human history. Of this self-righteous group,
Jesus said,

> Woe to you scribes and Pharisees, hypocrites, for you are like white washed tombs which on the outside appear beautiful, but inside they are full of dead men's bones and all uncleanness. So you, too, outwardly appear righteous to men, but inwardly you are full of hypocrisy and lawlessness. (Matthew 23:27-28).

The most religious people of His day considered themselves acceptable to God; yet Jesus defined them as unacceptable and unrighteous. They appeared clean on the exterior while internally, they were filthy, defiled and unrighteous. They needed the internal change that all men need. They needed to be born again. Speaking to His disciples about the Pharisees, Jesus said, "For I say to you that unless your righteousness surpasses that of the scribes and Pharisees, you will not enter the kingdom of heaven" (Matthew 5:20). They needed internal change and righteousness. An outward show of righteousness was insufficient, no matter how religious they appeared.

The professing Christian who is struggling with addiction should first determine with absolute certainty that he has been born again. He should confirm within himself that he has something more than mere religion. He should qualify himself in determining the inside of his person has been supernaturally transformed by the power of God. The Christian should have a witness of the Spirit, defining him as a true child of God. "The Spirit Himself testifies with our spirit that we are children of God" (Romans 8:16). In His message to the church at Ephesus, Jesus exhorted the church. "But I have this against you, that you have left your first love. Therefore, remember from where you have fallen, and repent and do the deeds you did at first" (Revelation 2:4-5).

The professing Christian struggling with addiction that cannot say with certainty he has been born again, should back up and begin with freedom step one. He should proceed forward and follow through with the remaining nine steps of freedom. If the struggling Christian knows for certain he is a legitimate child of God, he needs to recognize his sin, repent, ask God's forgiveness, and pray for deliverance. This will remove the obstacle of broken fellowship, cleanse the heart, and renew a right spirit. This is what David prayed and experience when he cried out to God after sinning. "Create in me a clean heart, O God, and renew a steadfast spirit within me" (Psalm 51:10). The Christian can then persevere and move forward with a diligent quest for victory. Keep going when you stumble; and arise when you fall. "For a righteous man falls seven times, and rises again" (Proverbs 24:16). The true child of God has been made and declared righteous by God. Settle that fact in your heart and mind, for God cannot lie. (Titus 1:2). Righteousness is a forever done deal for those who have truly received Christ. Regardless of how many times you may fall, God will see you through. Pursue deliverance by throwing yourself upon the complete mercy and grace of God. Never forget, God understands your battle. He loves you, will be with you, and will see you through until the end. God will never forsake His children!

Paul's letter to the Corinthians is positive proof that sometimes God's children struggle with sin. Paul himself admitted of not having arrived at a point of perfection. He acknowledged that he was not without sin and found himself struggling at times. "For what I am doing, I do not understand; for I am not practicing what I would like to do, but I am doing the very thing I hate" (Romans 7:15). To the Corinthians who did not always demonstrate the godly behavior of saints, Paul writes, "Such were some of you; but you were washed, but you were sanctified, but you were justified in the name of the Lord Jesus Christ and in the Spirit of our God" (1 Corinthians 6:11).

If you're a genuine born-again Christian struggling with addiction or any other sin, you need to understand who and what you are in Christ, and seize the victory by faith. Understand God in Christ has set you free and the power to overcome resides within. God has given you power to resist sin; He has given you the ability to say no. The moment you were born again, you were washed, justified, and sanctified in legal terms. Rest assured; God is at work and transforming your legal status into a practical reality, even when it may not seem like it. It may take some time. What you spent many years destroying will not be repaired instantaneously. The Holy Spirit is working to bring about the manifestation of your washing and sanctification. Eventually you will see His workings in your practical everyday living. God's work is a progressive, transforming process and experience.

To be bothered by your sin is a good indication that God is effectively at work. If we are His children, He is diligently at work. The word of God and the indwelling Holy Spirit are His means of performing inward change. The new man must be fed the word of God and yield to the sanctifying work of the Spirit. The work of God often brings about struggle on the path of progress toward change. God's transforming and resurrection power is always a work in progress. We are vessels of clay, continually turning on the Potter's wheel of design.

The born-again man resides in an unredeemed vessel of clay, while the inner man has been washed, justified, and sanctified. God has promised we will one day possess a glorified body. Until then, we will sense and continue to struggle in a carnal vessel. The flesh will throw fits and demand its own way. It may scream for a drink, a drug, a cigarette, for sexual fulfillment beyond God's acceptable will, or a multitude of other fleshly desires. God has given the Christian power and ability to say no. He also knows and understands the heart when we fail to demonstrate perfection. Recognize the resurrection power of Christ residing within you. James gives instruction on dealing with temptation from Satan. Peter describes him as "a roaring lion, seeking someone to devour" (1Peter 5:8). James writes, "Submit therefore to God. Resist the devil and he will flee for you" (James 4:7). God calls on us to resist and put up a fight against the enemy of our freedom. The Christian is entangled in a spiritual war with battles raging within and without. To Timothy, Paul wrote:

> Suffer hardship with me, as a good soldier of Christ Jesus. No soldier in active service entangles himself in the affairs of everyday life, so that he may please the one who enlisted him as a soldier (2 Timothy 2:3-4).

One of the great battles every Christian undergoes is entanglement with the world. Victorious living calls on God's children to give up the world by abandoning its promises and offers. We have eternity to enjoy the pleasures and blessings of a new world to come. This current world is only temporary; it will pass. Why should we invest all of our time, energies and finances into that which will one day cease to exist? Learn to follow the command of Jesus in the godly counsel He provides.

> Do not store up for yourselves treasures on earth, where moth and rust destroy, and where thieves break in and steal. But store up for yourselves treasures in heaven, where neither moth nor rust destroys, and where thieves do not break in or steal; for where your treasure is, there your heart will be also (Matthew 6:19-21).

I personally followed after the world for ten years in failing to understand who I really was. I felt like the proverbial "fish out of the water," an oddball living in a strange and foreign land. I tried to fit in and be a part of the world's mold. I was torn and divided on the inside. There was a failure on my part to understand I had been born again and undergone a supernatural transformation as a child. I was attempting to be something I was not, always trying to be someone else. A sheep will never be content, satisfied and fulfilled while living in a hog pen. Eventually God opened my eyes, giving me insight into who I was and what had transpired within. Much of the knowledge shared in this book was gleaned from those many years of struggle and experience. When I came to understand who I was in Christ, let go of the world and determined to pursue God with all my heart, mind, and soul; truth, spiritual growth, maturity and development rose to the forefront of my existence.

In the 1960's and 1970's a generation of youth in America were obsessed with finding and discovering themselves. They struggled with who they were and for what purpose they existed. Unfortunately, they failed to find themselves and the result was a nation thrust into a spiraling cesspool of sin resulting in many current day consequences. This is the natural state of fallen man. He does not understand who and what he is. He refuses to hear God's prognosis of the problem and rejects the only prescribed medicine available to combat and overcome his spiritual illness.

You should place what God desires and wills at the top of your priorities. Remove your eyes from off the world and set them steadfast upon the kingdom of God. Conform to who and what God has designed you to be. As an ambassador to the world, He has commissioned you to live a holy and righteous life. The practice of wallowing in the hog pens of the world will never produce godly characteristics. You cannot be a child of God and be content while acting like the world. How often does what we watch on television, listen to on the radio and read in the media have an impact upon our fleshly desires?

Solomon dispensed a great deal of wisdom in Proverbs when he wrote, "Do not look on the wine when it is red, when it sparkles in the cup" (Proverbs 23:31). Sin has an enticing nature which seeks to allure its victims by various modes and methods. The Christian is no exception and is not exempt to fleshly allurement. Advertisers, Hollywood, the music industry, and the mass media have made billions by appealing to the various sinful lusts of men and women. The world is filled with expertise in knowing how to make it look, feel, smell, taste and sound so appetizing. Far too often the Christian fails to understand what he watches, listens to, and participates in, affects his unredeemed flesh to a large extent. John warns us of allowing the influence of the world to take root in our hearts.

> For all that is in the world, the lust of the flesh and the lust of the eyes and the boastful pride of life, is not from the Father, but is from the world. The world is passing away, and also its lusts; but the one who does the will of God lives forever (1 John 2:16-17).

Get your eyes off the things of the world. If you watch lustful movies, the flesh will scream with lust. If you listen to ungodly music and watch ungodly movies, your mind is going to be filled with ungodly thoughts. What does a computer program produce? It produces what is programmed. What will your mind produce? It will produce exactly what you program it to produce. Turn aside from the world, forsake it, and immerse yourself in the things of God.

Here is a great area of failure in the lives of many Christians. They ride the fence and seek to have the best of both worlds. The Christian cannot be possessed by the world and experience the freedoms afforded in Christ. Turn away from the world's philosophies and desires. Understand, if you have been born again, this world has nothing of any value to offer. It cannot fulfill and satisfy your internal need; only the things of God can sustain a creature of God. The world cannot give you the peace of God. "Peace I leave with you; my peace I give; not as the world gives do I give to you" (John 14:27). Having and experiencing all God desires for you will require abandonment of the world. Many professing Christians spend a lifetime chasing after the world, rather than submitting to Christ and seeking after the things of God. The result is a defeated, unfulfilled, and worldly life.

Satan cannot rob a Christian of eternal life, but he does often prevent a Christian from enjoying God's best. Why would a child of God settle for second place when he has already won? A child of God can be robbed of peace, joy, and fellowship with his Maker. Sin can also rob a believer of his spiritual, physical, and mental health. You cannot pour water into the gas tank of an automobile and expect it to run smoothly. A Christian involved in sin will suffer the consequences. You cannot fuel a divine creature with pollutants of the world and expect life to run as God designed it. The Christian walking out in front of a speeding automobile is no more exempt from harm than a lost sinner committing the same act. A true Christian who behaves so foolishly has an airbus ticket to heaven, while the sinner has a train ticket to judgment. Physical death will be the consequence for both. In doing so, God's child has forfeited the purpose and plan which God had purposed for him in the present age. He has missed God's best! God has a perfect plan and design for each of His children. A genuine Christian will never lose or forfeit eternal life, but his sin can and will have a negative impact on the quality of life during his earthly residency and ministry.

Regarding God's purpose and plan for each of our lives, the Scripture states, "For we are His workmanship, created in Christ Jesus for good works, which God prepared beforehand so that we would walk in them" (Ephesians 2:10.) Satisfaction and fulfillment for the Christian is discovered with implementation and involvement in the works God has prepared for him. To fulfill this work, the Christian must be diligent in resisting temptation, and be committed to obeying the Lord toward fulfillment of the mission. You cannot put the world before God and fulfill the mission for which you have been called. The mission requires our full attention, focus, commitment and allegiance. We are called to lose ourselves in Christ. You cannot be content by living as one addicted to the world; addiction to Christ is the ultimate path of freedom and victorious living.

A Christian will never be successful in his mission when serious sin is allowed to remain. It will eventually become a stumbling block to moving forward in spiritual maturity and fulfilling God's plan. God is patient, gracious, and merciful in waiting for us to move forward. Some of our progression comes via His sovereignty and some comes through our willful submission. Any man with a nicotine habit, alcohol habit, drug habit, or illicit sexual habit, will never accomplish the full work God has planned and designed. He must abstain from his sin. It's not only upon the full-time minister to whom God has a calling and divine work prepared. No Christian will ever succeed in the good works God has purposed until serious sin is dealt with and eliminated.

When the Christian refuses to deal with sin and eliminate it, God will in due time handle the issue by His method. It's far more beneficial to deal with sin and judge ourselves, than postpone and force God's hand. "But if we judged ourselves rightly, we would not be judged. But when we are judged, we are disciplined by the Lord so that we will not be condemned along with the world" (1 Corinthians 11:31). God gives His children ample time to deal with their sin. His patience far exceeds that of man and He has proven to be long suffering in His grace and mercy. He will show us areas in our lives that we must deal with. God knows the heart and will deal with each us accordingly. When we fail to give Him our best, God will deal with the issues. He will step in and discipline as necessary. It is far better to resolve the issue ourselves than wait for God to chasten us. God is not beyond allowing us to go our own way in an effort to teach us valuable lessons. This happens when we hold on to sin and continue in disobedience. The consequences of undisciplined behavior are inevitable and will be determined by His sovereignty. God has prepared a place for each of His children within the church and His kingdom. He is a God of design who performs all works with perfection. Any sin in our lives is serious; however, certain sins are more detrimental and of a greater hindrance to the mission than others. The greater the sin, the greater the hindrance in stifling the works that God has created us for.

God has already given His people the means of victory over sin. It's now our responsibility to initiate and apply it. The ultimate goal is to say no and maintain a steadfast mind. God defines it as sin! Recognize the hindrance and make a firm decision to put it behind you. Just do it! Throw the cigarettes, the booze, the pills, the rocks in the garbage and make the determination to be done with them. When an individual truly makes up his mind to quit, he will quit! Paul said, "I can do all things through Him who strengthens me" (Philippians 4:13). It was applicable to Paul and can be applied to all of God's true people. When it comes to dealing with and eliminating sin, the phrase "I can't," is unacceptable vocabulary. Eliminate those words from your thought process when in reference to the will of God. There is no excuse for saying, "I can't stop this sin." God has given you the power to accomplish it, and He never requires us to perform the impossible.

Many years ago, when I was called to preach, I smoked over a pack per day. I smoked cigarettes fourteen years and understood blowing smoke in people's face would be unbecoming of a minister. It was a habit not to be tolerated or accepted in the pulpit. The cigarettes had to go if I were to become an effective and productive minister of the gospel. Abstaining from the nicotine habit was an ongoing struggle and battle. The Christian must take his struggles and battles before God if he is going to be victorious. We need God's help in everything, and should humbly admit we can do nothing of ourselves. Even Jesus needed help in fulfilling the mission for which He came. Rarely are we good at humbling ourselves and admitting we need help.

You may have to pray and quit a thousand times before the victory is experienced. God will not allow us to receive or take the glory for His work. Don't deceive yourself by thinking you did the conquering. Be willing and quick to give God the credit and glory for all forward progress. You must be willing to give Him the praise for all accomplishments. I prayed many times for deliverance and help in overcoming the sin of polluting God's temple with smoke. I admitted my struggle and battle with the smoky stick resting between my two fingers. God eventually provided deliverance from fourteen years of addiction to nicotine. You must be willing to give it up! With God's help you can overcome anything contrary to His will. To this day there are times when I feel as if I could smoke a cigarette. Over the years and through Christ, I have become stronger and stronger in the power of resisting smoke. The period of time between dreams and cravings for a nicotine fix has expanded throughout the years. I do not remember the last dream about smoking or craving a cigarette. Make up your mind, say no, and resist the fleshly urges to give in and fall backward. Make up your mind to be what and who God has called you to be and never give up conquered territory.

God has promised, "You will seek Me and find Me when you search for Me with all your heart" (Jeremiah 29:13). Just how much are you desirous of deliverance? God asks us to invest all of our energies, ambitions and dreams into the kingdom of God. He requires one hundred percent of our commitment, effort and dedication. He will be satisfied with nothing less! If we desire God's blessing, we much give Him our best. Jesus Christ must be the central focus and theme of the believer's life. He has given us the greatest commandment of all in guiding us toward His will. "You shall love the Lord your God with all your heart and with all your soul, and mind" (Matthew 22:37).

Love God more than the sin holding you hostage. The victory Christ has provided cannot be experienced in fullness until there is complete surrender to His sovereign will, purpose, and plan. Give God your best and understand He knows your heart. Sin is rebellion, it's displeasing to God, and every effort should be made to eliminate it. The believer's purpose is to please and glorify God. Pleasing God requires obedience and glorifying Him requires us to shine with good works. A sober life free from bondage pleases and glorifies God. The only way and means of ever pleasing God, is to be obsessed with doing those things which please Him. Make the decision to start pleasing God today and put the past in the rear-view mirror. Choose to move forward in a life of holiness and obedience. This is where victory will be found for the Christian who struggles with major areas of sin.

Chapter 13
Finding an Acceptable Church

The victorious Christian desiring to experience God's best, will become deeply involved with a local body of believers. Church is not an option for the Christian seeking to obey God. Under the inspiration of the Holy Spirit, the author of Hebrews exhorted God's people. "Not forsaking our own assembling together, as is the habit of some, but encouraging one another, and all the more as you see the day drawing near" (Hebrews 10:25). Many professing believers have made the statement, "I don't have to attend church to be a Christian." If you're going to be a faithful, victorious, obedient child of God, you will need to attend a church where Jesus Christ is taught and preached. Church is a spiritual obligation to be taken very seriously. At the "Judgment Seat of Christ" (2 Corinthians 5:10), the Christian will be held accountable for his faithful service in the church. God established and ordained the church for a purpose, and His people are to be an integral part of it. When God's people deny their obligation of faithfulness to the church, they fail in living up to their full potential. The mission of the church is also hindered by those who refuse to obey God in this truth.

A Christian missing in action is comparable to missing stones in a building. God is building a kingdom made of living stones, and as part of His work, you're not insignificant. Each stone has been properly fitted to meet a specific need. The Bible refers to Christians as "living stones," with each stone having a proper positioning. "You also as living stones, are being built up as a spiritual house for a holy priesthood, to offer up spiritual sacrifices acceptable to God through Jesus Christ" (1 Peter 2:5).

The primary purpose of the church is to reach lost sinners with the redemptive message of Jesus Christ. He has commanded those who follow Him to "go therefore and make disciples of all the nations" (Matthew 28:27). If the disciple is going to demonstrate faithfulness to the call of God, he must be involved in the work of a local church. In addition to the proclamation of the gospel, the church is instrumental in the spiritual growth, development and maturity of God's children. The Christian who is not involved with membership in a local church is spiritually malnourished and deficient in spiritual strength. God's children have been called to serve and be actively involved in a local body. The refusal to become involved in the fellowship of God's people is blatant rebellion, and leaves one suspect as to their real spiritual condition.

How can a person claim to know and love God; yet refuse to be a part of His church? How can anyone claim to love their brothers and sisters in Christ without being an active member of the family? How can someone claim to be a Christian, claim obedience to Christ, and deny His work by refusing to be a part of it? If the Spirit of God indwells your earthen vessel, you should have a desire to obey God, and be faithful to a local assembly. The heart should yearn for continual uninterrupted fellowship with others in Christ. If you have been born again there is an obligation to obey God and become faithful to a local church.

A professing Christian with no desire to participate in God's work is questionable. To proclaim a born-again experience and possess no desire to be involved with the kingdom is abnormal. If you're a child of God you should be following the commands of Jesus Christ. "But seek first His kingdom and His righteousness" (Matthew 6:33). If you are lacking in kingdom desires, then perhaps you should follow Paul's instruction and make sure you're truly in the faith (2 Corinthians 13:5). A profession of faith that fails to produce love for the things of God and bring forth the fruit of repentance is not genuine faith. Biblical faith will always produce action and involvement in the kingdom of God. When God grows a tree, it produces fruit.

If you profess to be a Christian and are not actively involved in a local church, you should begin your search immediately. Pray and ask the Lord to help you find a God fearing, doctrinally sound, Bible believing church. Become a member and find your proper place of service in Christ. Get involved in serving the Lord and others. Becoming a faithful church member is essential to "putting on the mind of Christ" (1 Corinthians 2:16). Faithful church attendance is necessary in assisting you to follow God's command to subdue the old and manifest the new.

> That in reference to your former manner of life, you lay aside the old self which is being corrupted in according to the lust of deceit, and that you be renewed in the spirit of your mind, and put on the new self which in the likeness of God has been created in righteousness and holiness of the truth (Ephesians 4:21-24).

The refusal to join a local ministry is tantamount to rebellion. God has called us to a life of making ourselves available to Him and others. We must live in submission and obedience if we are going to experience His best.

We have established the fact that Christians should be actively involved in a local church. God makes this fact very clear. Church participation is a significant part of God's general and specific will. God hasn't appointed any lone rangers in the kingdom. A Christian who is physically able and not involved with a local church is simply outside the will of God. The church is God's means of ministry where His word is preached, taught, practiced, lived and proclaimed. The church is necessary for the spiritual growth and maturity of a believer.

Finding a true biblical based local assembly can prove to be a challenge. Don't be discouraged in your search. With a sincere effort bathed in prayer, and a diligent search, you will discover the fellowship God has for you. Don't be in a rush! Visit churches in your surrounding area and wait on God to show you His choice. God has faithful believers around the world. Before becoming involved and committed to a local church, the believer should confirm that leadership adheres to certain foundational truths. Sound doctrine is an absolute essential element of any acceptable local body of believers. There are some basic doctrinal truths required if a church is to be classified as a sound biblical assembly. Let's look at twelve major points which would point to a Bible believing, God fearing, doctrinally sound church.

First, a Bible believing church will preach and teach the Deity of the Lord Jesus Christ. This point expresses Jesus Christ as Almighty God who came to earth clothed in humanity. As God, He has always existed; He has neither beginning nor end. Jesus Christ is the Eternal God who has been given all authority in "heaven and on earth" (Matthew 28:27). In the Gospel of John, Jesus Christ is clearly revealed as to His identity. "In the beginning was the word, and the word was with God, and the word was God" (John 1:1). The Word of God left His heavenly home in the splendors of glory and came to earth as a man without ceasing to be God. The purpose of His coming was to redeem man from the law's curse and the penalty of sin. He came as a means of reuniting man with God. A true church will teach Jesus Christ was both fully God and man. "For in Him all the fullness of Deity dwells in bodily form" (Colossians 2:9). A genuine Christian must accept this essential doctrinal truth if he is going to demonstrate faithfulness to the true gospel. If a local church is to be worthy of commitment, it will adhere to this basic doctrine of the Christian faith. Make sure the pastor and leadership believe in the Deity of Jesus Christ before uniting with a local assembly.

Second, a Bible believing church will preach and teach the Trinity. The Scripture defines God as One, and yet seen in three Persons. This biblical fact is found in the Old Testament book of Deuteronomy, "Hear, O Israel" The Lord our God, is one" (Deuteronomy 6:4)! When we speak of the Trinity, we define God as being one, and yet existent in the three persons of the God-Head: The Father, the Son, and the Holy Spirit. In the Trinity we recognize One God, yet we see Him in three distinct Persons of the same essence. The word Trinity is not found in the Bible; however, the three Persons of the Trinity are clearly defined in the pages of Scripture. There are many passages where Trinitarian doctrine is evidenced, beginning with the book of Genesis. "Then God said, Let Us make man in Our image, according to Our likeness" (Genesis 1:26). In the word "Our," we recognize the God-Head conferring with one another. Depicting the water baptism of Jesus, the Scripture provides proof of the Trinity.

After being baptized, Jesus came up immediately from the water; and behold, the heavens were opened, and He saw the Spirit of God descending as a dove and lighting on Him, and behold, a voice out of the heavens said. "This is Mybeloved Son, in whom I am well pleased" (Matthew 3:16-17).

The Trinity is a necessary doctrine of any local assembly. God the Son is being baptized in water, the Holy Spirit descends upon Him as a dove, and the Father speaks from heaven. A local church or movement rejecting the Trinity should be avoided. Movements and preachers in denial of the Trinity should be rejected by any truth- seeking child of God. A sound biblical minister and congregation will espouse Trinitarian teaching.

Third, a Bible believing church will proclaim and teach the virgin birth of Jesus Christ. If Jesus was not born of a virgin, He has no claim to Deity. He could not have been God incarnate but for this fact. Hundreds of years before Christ came to earth, the Old Testament prophet Isaiah foretold of a coming Messiah who would be conceived of a virgin. "Therefore, the Lord Himself shall give you a sign: Behold, a virgin will be with child and bear a son, and she will call His name Immanuel" (Isaiah 7:14).

In order to fulfill the Old Testament prophecy, the Christ child would have to be born of a virgin. The New Testament confirms Christ was brought forth from the womb of a virgin in fulfillment of this Old Testament prophecy.

> Now all this took place to fulfill what was spoken by the Lord through the prophet: "Behold, the virgin shall be with child and shall bear a son, and they shall call His name Immanuel," which translated means, "God with us" (Matthew 1:22-23).

The sinful nature of man was passed down from the seed of his ancestral father Adam. All men have inherited the corrupt nature of Adam; therefore, they are born under a curse of death. The Scripture tells us Jesus was not born of Adam's seed, but was born of God as "The only begotten Son of God (John 3:16). The Gospel of Luke identifies Jesus as being conceived of the Holy Spirit.

> The angel answered and said to her, "The Holy Spirit will come upon you, and the power of the Most High will overshadow you; and for that reason the holy Child shall be called the Son of God" (Luke 1:35).

As the Son of God, Jesus did not inherit the sinful nature of man as passed down by Adam. The Bible is clear on this point in that Jesus never sinned. "He made Him who knew no sin to be sin on our behalf, so that we might become the righteousness of God in Him" (2 Corinthians 5:21). Jesus was absolute sinless perfection birthed in human flesh through a virgin. When He died on the cross, He became sin for the sinner and now offers man His perfect righteousness. "But God demonstrates His love toward us, in that while we were yet sinners, Christ died for us" (Romans 5:8). Any church, preacher, or teacher refusing to recognize and proclaim the virgin birth of Jesus Christ, is not worthy of your attention. The virgin birth of Jesus Christ is defined as an essential and necessary doctrine of the Christian faith.

Fourth, a Bible believing church will teach the death, burial, and resurrection of Jesus Christ. The Christian must believe Jesus Christ died on the cross in paying the penalty of man's sin, was buried in a tomb, and resurrected from the dead. Through His death the works of the devil have been destroyed. "Therefore, since the children share in flesh and blood, He Himself likewise also partook of the same, that through death He might render powerless him who had the power of death, that is, the devil" (Hebrews 2:14).

The power of death reigned over man until Christ died on the cross. Through His sacrificial death on the cross, life is offered to all who will accept His gift by faith. Paul provides us with the rest of the story in his letter to the Corinthians. "For I delivered to you as of first importance what I also received, that Christ died for our sins according to the Scriptures, and that He was buried, and that He was raised on the third day according to the Scriptures" (1 Corinthians 15:3-4).

The death, burial, and resurrection of Jesus Christ, is considered an essential doctrine of the Christian faith. The resurrection is foundational to Christianity and serves to prove Jesus was who and all He claimed to be. Without the death, burial and resurrection of Christ, there is no true biblical faith. Jesus is known in Scripture as "the author and finisher of our faith" (Hebrews 12:2 KJV). Christ founded and established the basic teachings of the church. He trained others to carry on and build "on the foundation of the apostles and prophets, Christ Jesus Himself being the corner stone" (Ephesians

2:20). This is a necessary element of the gospel and must be maintained at all costs. Any church or minister rejecting this important teaching is unworthy of any Christian's attention.

Fifth, a Bible believing church will teach man is born into the world as a sinner, spiritually dead, unclean, and spiritually defiled in the eyes of God. Through Adam, everyone born into this world is cursed. The natural born man is portrayed as being under the wrath of God. Unless he undergoes a spiritual change of which only God can initiate, he will die in his sin and be confined to a place of eternal suffering. God's word is definitively clear on this subject, "For all have sinned and fall short of the glory of God" (Romans 3:23). God's word has established all as guilty before God in regard to sin and in need of forgiveness. Paul further tells us, "For the wages of sin is death" (Romans 6:23). To the Galatians he wrote, "But the Scripture has shut up everyone under sin" (Galatians 3:22). Speaking of those who have been born again, Paul stressed, "And you who were dead in your trespasses and sins" (Ephesians 2:1). Man is a sinner and needs to fall upon the extended grace and mercy of God. Any church neglecting the reality of man's sinfulness and need for redemption is unworthy of the redeemed.

Sixth, a Bible believing assembly will teach salvation from eternal destruction is acquired only by faith in the Person of Jesus Christ and the atoning work of the cross. Salvation is received by faith alone. "For by grace you have been saved through faith; and that not of yourselves, it is the gift of God; not as a result of works, so that no one may boast" (Ephesians 2:8-9).

Man's own works and efforts can play no part in his salvation. God's grace is strictly a gift and cannot be earned or merited. Not only is the Christian saved by God's grace, he remains saved and is kept by grace. Once a person has truly received God's gift of salvation, it can never be lost, forfeited, or destroyed. Eternal security is the promise and assurance of God's word to all who receive Christ as Lord and Savior by faith. Man is neither saved nor kept by his own works. A biblically sound church will teach salvation is by grace alone through faith in the Lord Jesus Christ.

Seventh, a Bible believing church will proclaim the necessity of the new birth. Spiritual birth is essential to man's salvation and deliverance. Jesus answered and said to him, "Truly, truly, I say to you, unless one is born again he cannot see the kingdom of God" (John 3:3). To be born again is to experience a supernatural spiritual transformation. The new birth can only be acquired by repentance (turning from sin), and accepting Jesus Christ as Lord and Savior by faith. Man is born into this world of Adam, possessing a sin nature and deemed as unfit for the kingdom of God. The Almighty will not allow man into His eternal kingdom as a creature of sin. Man's only hope is the new birth offered by Christ, which is imperative to biblical Christianity. Man is born physically of Adam, he is born spiritually of Christ; hence, he must be born again. Those who have not experienced the new birth are spiritually dead. Any legitimate Bible believing ministry will compel men to be born again.

Eighth, a Bible believing church will teach Jesus Christ as the only means of attaining a right relationship with God, and declare all other ways to be false. Jesus defined Himself as "the resurrection and the life" (John 11:25). He declared there is no other way or means of salvation and deliverance from sin. "I am the way, and the truth, and the life; no one comes to the Father but through Me" (John 14:7). As a leader in the early church, Peter expounded on this truth with clarity; "And there is salvation in no one else; for there is no other name under heaven that has been given among men by which we must be saved (Acts 4:12)." Any organization, movement, or church denying Jesus Christ as the only way and means of salvation should be avoided at all costs. Spiritual deliverance is available only in the redemptive work of Christ.

Ninth, a Bible believing church will teach the Bible to be the written word of God. The Scriptures will be defined as inspired, inerrant and infallible. They should be upheld as the sole authority with regard to doctrine, and the only standard for Christian living. The word of God admonishes us, "All Scripture is inspired by God and profitable for teaching, for reproof, for correction" (2 Timothy 3:16). Any other works claiming to be inspired of God should be recognized as false.

I testify to everyone who hears the words of the prophecy of this book: if anyone adds to them, God will add to him the plagues which are written in this book; and if anyone takes away from the words of the book of this prophecy, God will take away his part from the tree of life and from the holy city, which are written in this book (Revelation 22:18-19).

Any movement claiming to have revelation beyond what is already provided in the word of God should be avoided. Any pastor, teacher or church touting new revelation beyond what's already found in the Bible should be renounced as false. The Bible is the only literary work worthy of a claim to divine inspiration. Avoidance should be the attitude toward any church, group, movement, or individual daring to claim divine inspiration beyond the printed word of God.

Tenth, a Bible believing church will teach Jesus Christ is literally coming back to receive His people and judge the world. Jesus came the first time with the purpose of defeating death, sin, Satan, the grave, and to provide man a way of escaping eternal damnation. The Bible gives God's people this certain assurance. This same Jesus who once walked the shores of Galilee will return to set up a literal righteous kingdom on earth. The Christian should be longing for and awaiting His arrival. As Jesus ascended back into heaven, the disciples were given this promise of God. They also said, "Men of Galilee, why do you stand looking into the sky? This Jesus, who has been taken up from you into heaven, will come in just the same way as you have watched Him go into heaven" (Acts 1:11). From the very lips of Jesus came these words. "And then the sign of the Son of Man will appear in the sky, and then all the tribes of the earth will mourn, and they will see the Son of Man coming on the clouds of the sky with power and great glory" (Matthew 24:30). The Scripture is replete with promises and assurances of His return. A sound doctrinal church will teach the literal Second Coming of Jesus Christ to set up a righteous kingdom on earth. The kingdom of God has already been established in the hearts of His people. The Christian should refuse to participate with any assembly rejecting the literal Second Coming of Christ.

Eleventh, a Bible believing church will teach the existence of a literal heaven and hell. Jesus defined Himself as "the living bread that came down out of heaven" (John 6:51). How could He have come from heaven, if heaven does not actually exist? In "The Revelation of Jesus Christ," John said he "saw heaven opened" (Revelation 19:11). There is an existent heavenly realm; a heaven which cannot be seen with the natural or naked eye. Heaven is a literal place where God the Father, God the Son, angels, and those who have died in Christ now reside. The Bible tells us Jesus "has been given all authority in heaven and on earth" (Matthew 28:18). Heaven is a place where no sin, sickness, sorrow, death or evil exists. Here is another great and precious promise of God's word.

"And He will wipe away every tear from their eyes; and there will no longer be any death; there will no longer be any mourning, or crying, or pain; the first things have passed away" (Revelation 21:4). Jesus prayed, "Your will be done on earth as it is in heaven" (Matthew 6:10). Just as planet earth can be defined as a material location, heaven is occupied and declared as an existent place in the spiritual realm. The apostle Paul describes this place as "the third heaven" (2 Corinthians 12:2-4).

> I know a man in Christ who fourteen years ago, whether in the body I do not know, or out of the body I do not know, God knows such a man was caught up to the third heaven. And I know how such a man, whether in the body or apart from the body I do not know, God knows, was caught up into Paradise and heard inexpressible words, which a man is not permitted to speak.

Paul is speaking of a definitive place called heaven and a reality not to be denied by a true Bible believing assembly of believers. It's a place filled with God's glory, perfection, peace, joy and righteousness. Heaven is a place of absolute purity, holiness, and unity, where no evil resides. God has promised an eternal home in heaven for all who will come to Jesus Christ by faith.

On the opposite end of eternity is a bottomless pit of judgment. Jesus had much to say about this abode of eternal suffering. Perhaps the most vivid illustration of hell is portrayed by Jesus in a story of the rich man and Lazarus. Lazarus went to enjoy the presence of God in a place called Paradise; the rich man having died in sin, made his eternal abode in hell.

> Now the poor man died and was carried away by the angels to Abraham's bosom; and the rich man also died and was buried. In Hades he lifted up his eyes, being in torment; and saw Abraham far away and Lazarus in his bosom. And he cried out and said, "Father Abraham, have mercy on me, and send

Lazarus so that he may dip the tip of his finger in water and cool off my tongue, for I am in agony in this flame." But Abraham said, "Child, remember that during your life you received your good things, and likewise Lazarus bad things; but now he is being comforted here, and you are in agony" (Luke 16:23-24).

Hell is not a place to be taken lightly. It's certainly no joke! God has no desire to see people confined in this pit of human suffering. His will for men is to repent and accept His gracious offer of salvation. "The Lord is not slow about His promise, as some count slowness, but is patient toward you, not wishing for any to perish but for all to come to repentance" (2 Peter 3:9). The Scripture warns man of this final place of torment for lost men, rebellious angels and Satan. In finality, it is defined as "the Lake of Fire."

Then death and Hades were thrown into the lake of fire. This is the second death, the lake of fire. And if anyone's name was not found written in the book of life, he was thrown into the lake of fire (Revelation 20:14-15).

God does not take it upon Himself to warn men of imaginary places. All men who reject Jesus Christ as Lord and Savior will spend eternity in a literal place of eternal suffering. In the Lake of Fire, man will be separated from God and all that is good forever. Eternal punishment will not be a party as some like to jokingly mock. Hell will be a place of eternal confinement; a place where no fun, pleasure, joy, peace, contentment, companionship, fellowship or fulfillment will ever be experienced. An eternal separation from the things of God will be finalized. Any church sanctioned by Jesus Christ will acknowledge the existence of a literal heaven and hell.

Twelfth, a Bible believing church will teach eternal security for the believer. In common church vernacular this is known as "once saved always saved." Great peace is found, afforded and experienced in the assurance of eternal life that is unending, everlasting and secure in Christ. Eternal life can only be defined as eternal and by nature everlasting. If eternal life is everlasting, it cannot be lost. This is the divine life created by God when an individual is born again. God cannot die; therefore, the divine nature created by God cannot be destroyed. Jesus speaks of the believer as having become one with Him. "That they also may be one; even as You, Father, are in Me and I in You, that they also may be in Us" (John 17:21). Those who are one with God cannot be separated from Him. The eternal life given by God will endure forever, it is indestructible. Paul wrote, "Therefore there is now no condemnation for those who are in Christ Jesus" (Romans 8:1). Once a person is "in Christ," there is no means, method or way to be severed from His power to keep us.

> For I am convinced that neither death, nor life, nor angels, nor principalities, nor things present, nor things to come, nor powers, nor height, nor depth, nor any other created thing, will be able to separate us from the love of God, which is in Christ Jesus our Lord (Romans 8:38-39).

Nothing will ever separate a genuine believer from the love of his Heavenly Father. There is no severing of this everlasting relationship between a born-again believer and Jesus Christ. God saves and keeps those who come to Him. The eternal security received in Christ cannot be lost, forfeited, returned, or destroyed by any means. The individual who is genuinely transformed in Christ is utterly incapable of reversing what has begun. He has become an eternal member of a kingdom of which there is no way out. A sound biblical based church will teach God's precious gift to man is eternally secure in Christ. One would be wise to refrain from committing to movements who reject God's ability to keep those He saves. When there is no eternal security, there is no consistent peace and certainty.

As an ordained Southern Baptist pastor, I would highly recommend membership in a conservative Southern Baptist Church. However, due diligence is required even among Southern Baptist fellowships. There are some liberal, left-wing leaning elements among our own ranks. Spiritual liberalism in churches is defined as those guilty of compromising and watering down the word of God. Some would dare to deny the inerrant, infallible, and inspired claims of Scripture. Liberal elements of the Southern Baptist ranks should be avoided at all costs. A watered-down message has no power to save and transform.

On the other end of the line is extremism. Churches and movements crossing acceptable lines will eventually lead people into legalism. This problem is less likely found in the Southern Baptist ranks. I would strongly suggest a conservative Southern Baptist fellowship which adheres to the doctrinal issues set forth in the preceding paragraphs. Meet with the pastor and discuss these issues in pursuit of a church home. Take time to converse with deacons and other church members to ascertain the doctrinal beliefs and teachings of the church. They should adhere to The Baptist Faith and Message statement as upheld by the Southern Baptist Convention. The new Christian attending church will be hard pressed to discern the foundational teachings of a church simply by visiting a couple of times. Ask for doctrinal materials of churches you may visit. Make sure they have a doctrinal statement of faith espousing with clarity what they believe.

I consider myself a well-rounded, balanced, and very conservative Southern Baptist minister. I spent ten years in the Pentecostal and Charismatic movements where I discovered some troubling doctrines and purported manifestations of the Holy Spirit. Many of these manifestations cannot be justified within the pages of Scripture. Be very weary of movements stressing sensationalism, signs, miracles, healings, supernatural manifestations, and wonders. Do we serve a supernatural God? Yes! Is God in the wholesale signs and wonders miracle business? No! Is God in the business of dispensing new revelatory information not already revealed in Scripture? No! Stay away from churches, movements, and ministers who make a practice of these elements.

While there are born again believers in many of these movements who possess a true love for God, I cannot with good conscious recommend a church among their ranks. These movements can be just as harmful as many of the liberal elements within professing Christianity. They have become playgrounds of Satan, the master of deception. He has built many nests among God's professing people in this present church age. Spiritual deception runs rampant across the United States and around the world. Jesus warned of a coming day of great deception when He said, "For false Christ's and false prophets will arise and will show great signs and wonders, so as to mislead, if possible, even the elect" (Matthew 24:24). Those days are upon us and rapidly approaching their peak. Satan often uses such movements in seeking to lead God's people astray with emotionalism, false teaching, sensationalism and mesmerism.

Beyond aberrant teachings in conservative circles of the church are also those elements making up the liberal movements of professing Christianity. They have compromised and rendered the word of God ineffective with watered down gospels, and have accepted sinful lifestyles contrary to the word of God. Stay away from organizations guilty of sanctioning homosexual marriage and ordination. Avoid institutions that deny their ministers the right to marry. Many of the once great denominations of the world have fallen into apostasy and are guilty of leading people away from the true Christ of Scripture. The religious world is filled with landmines of falsehood. For the most part, these religious institutions have gone astray regarding the essential doctrines of the faith mentioned above.

The believer should be very careful regarding independent movements and churches. One of the great problems among independents is often a lack of leadership accountability. While there are perhaps some very good Independent Bible believing churches, many of them present reasons for concern. Make sure the doctrinal teachings of the word of God are of a foremost priority in the ministry of leadership and church government. The pastor should be held accountable by those he serves.

The professing church of this day has become a nest for all types. It has become a tree producing both bad and good fruit. Find a church filled with the good fruits of God's word and His Spirit. Be diligent in your search for a doctrinally sound, biblically based church.

Conclusion

There is an abundant supply of hope and promise for the addict who desires change. As a twelve-year old child, Jesus sat in the synagogue and spoke to the people.

> The Spirit of the Lord is upon Me, because He has anointed Me to preach the gospel to the poor. He has sent Me to proclaim release to the captives, and recovery of sight to the blind, to set free those who are oppressed (Luke 4:18).

Few scriptures would so aptly illustrate the lost condition of an addict bound by his addiction. Many addicts are living in spiritual and monetary poverty as a result of their bondage. Every dime is often spent on the cravings of their addiction. The addict is often a poor manager of his financial resources due to the foolish behavior produced by his habit. Many addicts are all too familiar with a broken heart, not to mention the number of hearts he has broken along the path of destruction. Undoubtedly, the addict is held captive by a power beyond his own control. He is enslaved to the cry and demands of his master. He lives for another fix, another drunk, another binge, or for his next drug crazed spree. Over and over again he lives to regret his actions. He is always looking back, experiencing the inevitable pain, suffering, woe, misery, and a haunting voice of the past. Oh, "if I could only go back and undue my past, I would do things so differently?" Living in the past only serves as a cage for the future.

The addict is blind and oblivious as to what is happening. He is even less concerned about the problems of those around him. As with all sinners, the addict needs his spiritual eyes and ears opened to the truth. He is in dire need of relief from the insanity and spiritual illness plaguing his soul. He desperately needs to experience the blessing of God's amazing grace and His gracious power to restore sight. His ears miraculously need to hear the voice of God saying, "This is the way, walk in it" (Isaiah 30:21). The addict needs deliverance such as few would understand. He lives from day to day as a fish on a hook, always fighting and never brought to shore. His mouth is sore from the flesh hooks holding him captive. He is often bruised and beaten from the raging battle churning deep within the recesses of his heart, soul, and mind. Although seldom or never admitted, he yearns to be set at liberty from the destructive force of deep darkness that clouds his mind.

Jesus Christ offers freedom from addiction. Enslavement to alcohol and drugs is a tormenting nightmare defined as bondage to a cruel taskmaster. The root of addiction is sin, and freedom is found only in its eradication. The Great Physician longs to extract this cancerous illness eating away at deprived humanity. Jesus makes it abundantly clear, "So if the Son makes you free, you will be free indeed" (John 8:36). Freedom is found in following after the One who authored and won freedom for all who would call on Him. There is no proven earthly remedy for the scourge of addiction. Worldly programs have experienced a dismal failure rate, but a supernatural remedy is available for those who will receive Him. The world emphatically declares and denies the existence of a cure for this problem. God disputes the world's professional claims when he declares:

> For the wisdom of this world is foolishness before God. For it is written, He is the one who catches the wise in their craftiness; and again, the Lord knows the reasoning of the wise, that they are useless (1 Corinthians 3:19-20).

There is an effective cure and deliverance from addiction when God's prescription is properly received and applied. The world denies a cure for addiction and God balks at their foolishness. The once addicted who has experienced the life changing power of God understands that Jesus Christ sets the captive free. There is a cure! Those who partake of this remedy will never again be required to sit at a roundtable and declare; "my name is Mike and I'm an addict," or "my name is Mike and I'm an alcoholic." A born-again Christian is able to hold his head high and proclaim it from the housetops, "I have become a new creature in Christ, I have been forever set free by the resurrection power of God and the Holy Spirit who dwells within." He can arrive at a solemn place of security in Christ whereby it may be said, "thank God, I have recovered from the addiction which once enslaved me." He can stand clean before the world and God while proclaiming, "Therefore if anyone is in Christ, he is a new creature; the old things passed away; behold, new things have come" (2 Corinthians 5:17).

Notice what Paul says to some Corinthians who experienced a problem with addiction and were referred to as drunkards. "Such were some of you; but you were washed, but you were sanctified, but you were justified in the name of the Lord Jesus Christ and in the Spirit of our God" (1 Corinthians 6:11). These drunkards had been washed and cleansed of their sin. They were free from defilement; and no longer unclean or unfit to experience a righteous relationship with God. Drunkards who had been delivered, sanctified and set aside for God's will. There is a new life awaiting the addict who will immerse himself in God's Addiction Recovery Plan and follow The Biblical Path to Freedom by applying biblical truth to his life. He can be clean and set free from the fleshly hooks of addiction by throwing himself at the feet of a merciful and gracious God.

This book will be deemed contrary to the ways, means, assessments, diagnosis, prognosis, conclusions and philosophies of the world. The present order of this world runs backward with regard to the thoughts and ways of God. It does not and cannot understand spiritual truth. How can the people of this world accurately diagnose and resolve a spiritual problem, when they themselves are "dead in trespasses and sins" (Ephesians 2:1)? Only those connected with God can understand spiritual issues. "But a natural man does not accept the things of the Spirit of God, for they are foolishness to him; and he cannot understand them, because they are spiritually appraised" (1 Corinthians 2:14).

Those born of this world who have not received God's blessing of redemption are defined by Paul as the natural man. One of man's greatest stumbling blocks is an attitude of believing that he knows more than God. In his natural fallen state, man is void of divine knowledge and wisdom. He cannot know and comprehend truth because he does understand the things of God. The Psalmist warns the wise of worldly wisdom and counsel by declaring,

How blessed is the man who does not walk in the counsel of the wicked, nor stand in the path of sinners, nor sit in the seat of scoffers! But his delight is in the law of the LORD, and in His law he meditates day and night. He will be like a tree firmly planted by streams of water, which yields its fruit in its season and its leaf does not wither; and in whatever he does, he prospers (Psalm 1:1-3).

Those who study psychology, psychiatry and sociology may understand some aspects of the natural man; but when dealing the spiritual aspects of man, they are empty and void of wisdom. The world's wisdom is incapable of effectively dealing with the spiritual part of man known and understood only by God. When man has a physical problem, he should perhaps consult a professional familiar with the physical body. When he needs financial investment advice, he should visit a professional financial adviser. When a man is confronted with a spiritual problem, he should consult the word of God and seek counsel from a man of God who can provide knowledge and wisdom on spiritual matters.

For the word of the cross is foolishness to those who are perishing, but to us who are being saved it is the power of God. For it is written "I will destroy the wisdom of the wise, and the cleverness of the clever I will set aside." Where is the wise man? Where is the scribe? Where is the debater of this age? Has not God made foolish the wisdom of the world (1 Corinthians 1:18-20).

At the root of addiction resides a spiritual problem. Despite the world's claim of knowledge on this subject, addiction is not a physical illness someone is born with. It is the cause of much physical, mental, emotional, and spiritual illness; however, the root cause of addiction is a spiritual problem called sin. Unless an addict deals with the underlying problem of sin, his addiction will never be fully conquered. This is why the philosophy of worldly counsel can only provide the assertion, "once an addict always an addict," and "once an alcoholic, always an alcoholic."

It should be noted that alcohol is simply another drug. The only difference between alcohol and drugs is the issue of legality. Alcohol is a legal substance in most countries and has an extreme negative effect upon those who abuse it. The abuse of legal prescription drugs has the same impact as abuse of illegal drugs. Drugs are no respecter of persons when it comes to addiction. They attack rich, poor, black, white, male and female. It's a universal tragedy and epidemic. The same root cause is discovered at the foundation of each wreck. These are lives built on sinking foundations and sands of sin. The addict as well as all others would do well to absorb the words of wisdom coming from the Son of God who once walked the shores of Galilee. Regardless of how educated, religious and wise the man of this world may be, he will never match the wisdom and instruction of the King and Creator of the universe.

> Therefore, everyone who hears these words of mine and acts on them may be compared to a wise man who built his house on the rock. And the rain fell, and the floods came, and the winds blew and slammed against that house; and yet it did not fall, for it had been founded on the rock. Everyone who hears these words of mine and does not act on them will be like a foolish man who built his house on the sand. The rain fell, and the floods came, and the winds blew and slammed against that house; and it fell and great was its fall. When Jesus had finished these words, the crowds were amazed at His teaching; for He was teaching them as one having authority, and not as their scribes (Matthew 7:24-29).

Man is longing for happiness, contentment, joy, peace and righteousness. He seeks after these longings by various means with great effort. In spiritual deafness, and blindness he somehow believes these blessings can be found in fame, fortune, fulfillment of desire, entertainment and material possessions. Happy hour is a national anticipation for many who need a drink to calm their nerves and sooth the stress of a difficult day. Lottery lines can be witnessed in convenience stores every Saturday evening. The registers are surrounded by those who believe winning the lotto is the answer and solution to all of their earthly problems, needs and desires. Reality shows abound with idolaters seeking fame, fortune and notoriety. The lost man is ruled by the misleading desires of his corrupted heart. The answer to mans need for release from stress, bondage and enslavement is found in Paul's writings to the church at Ephesus. "So then, do not be foolish, but understand what the will of the Lord is, and do not get drunk with wine, for that is dissipation, but be filled with the Spirit" (Ephesians 5:18).

Men earnestly believe they can find satisfaction, contentment and peace in alcohol, drugs, entertainment, sports, material goods, and a plethora of other things. His mind is inebriated with the stinky thinking of the world. He is obsessed with the idea of a utopian world able to provide him with the inner satisfaction and fulfillment he is ultimately seeking. Paul says only the Spirit of God can satisfy the deepest longings of a man's empty soul. In his letter to the Romans he expresses the true need and desire of the human heart and where it can be discovered; "For the kingdom of God is not eating and drinking but righteousness and peace and joy in the Holy Spirit" (Romans 14:17).

Alcohol and drugs are used as a substitute, an attempt to replace and accomplish what only the Spirit of God can do for a lost man's soul. Herein resides the great problem of obtaining counsel from those who do not know and promote the ways of God. The psychologists and psychiatrists may be able to deal with certain issues of the human body and brain; however, they are void of counsel in dealing with the spiritual issues and aspects of God's truth. Only God can meet the true need of a man's spiritual heart.

Man was created by God. The Creator knows and understands what will best satisfy and meet the needs of His creation. An automobile sputters and runs at less than full power when its fuel is defiled and polluted by a foreign substance. When a manufacturer builds a quality piece of complicated machinery, it develops an operation manual to provide intricate details of its operation and function. In order for the machinery to be properly maintained and operated, the manual must be followed. In many cases the warranty of equipment is voided when manual procedures are not adhered to. God has provided His creation with a service manual called the Bible.

This inspired instruction booklet is the very word of God. Man will never be what God intended unless he follows the manual of life so graciously bestowed upon him. Man will never experience true satisfaction, fulfillment, contentment, peace, joy and righteousness outside of a relationship with Jesus Christ. He cannot deny his Creator and function properly in a vessel marred by a corrupt nature. His life will never operate as it was intended until he turns toward the Great Manufacturer in the heavens who created man and the marvelous universe he resides in.

Jesus Christ is the perfect illustration of what God desires for man. He was perfect, sinless, and void of any spot or blemish. God's only standard of acceptance is perfection; hence, man in his imperfect condition is at odds and hostile toward his Creator. God's desire for all is to be like Christ. "As is the earthy, so also are those who are earthy; and as is the heavenly, so also are those who are heavenly. Just as we have borne the image of the earthy, we will also bear the image of the heavenly" (1Corinthians 15:48-49).

Jesus is the perfect example of the heavenly. He came from heaven where He existed for all eternity before entering into human history and walking in flesh upon this darkened planet corrupted by sin. In His claim to Deity, He provides man with what is needed to survive the coming judgment; "For the bread of God is that which comes down from heaven and gives life to the world" (John 6:33).

Jesus came bearing the image of the heavenly. If man is to ever experience and see the portals of heaven, he must also bear the image of the heavenly. God has made it abundantly clear! There will be no room in heaven for those who are not conformed to His heavenly standard of perfection. The only means of transformation is the supernatural act of a spiritual birth. Only God can transform man into a divine heavenly creature made fit for an eternal home in heaven.

Can you say with absolute certainty at this point, "I have been born again and become a child of God?" Can you proclaim with a divine witness that should you die today you would arrive and break through to a heavenly destination? God makes it clear, you can know with absolute certainty a heavenly home awaits your arrival. "These things I have written to you who believe in the name of the Son of God, so that you may know that you have eternal life" (1 John 5:13).

If you have never made the decision to accept Jesus Christ as your personal Lord and Savior, you should take an eternal step of faith at this time. It's a simple and profound life changing decision. To take this life changing step requires meaning business with God. You must be willing to give up your own life in exchange for the life He has designed and planned for you. If you are ready and willing to make this crucial decision, please pray the following prayer and mean it with all of your being, from the deep recesses of your heart.

Dear God in heaven. I come to you in the name of Jesus Christ. I confess I am a sinner in need of salvation from sin. I need the forgiveness and deliverance only you can provide. At this moment, I have decided to repent, turn from my sin, turn from the world, and turn to Jesus Christ by faith. I acknowledge Jesus Christ was God in the flesh; He died on the cross for my sin, and arose from the dead. Lord Jesus, I confess with my mouth you are the One and Only true God. I ask you to forgive me of all my sin, wash me, and make me a new creature through the new birth. I agree to give up my own life and become all you would desire of me. Lord, I invite and ask you into my life as Lord and Savior. Lord, thank you for coming into my life. Take me and do with me as you will. I will submit to your will, purpose, and plan from this day forward. Please help me to persevere in my commitment and enable me overcome my weaknesses and failures – Amen.

If you have prayed this prayer and truly meant it with all of your heart, welcome to the family of God. You have become a born again Christian and are safely secure in the powerful arms of Jesus Christ. You have been forgiven of all your sins: past, present, and future. You have begun a spiritual journey and adventure that will one day usher you into the eternal presence of God. You are now His child, a member of the kingdom, and a member of His universal church. You are blessed and have received the free gift of eternal life.

It's time to surround yourself with people and places who will be instrumental in helping you in your new walk. Find a good church home, settle down and surround yourself with godly people. Prayer, Bible study, and Christian fellowship will help you along The Biblical Path to Freedom. Be diligent in your quest for truth. A life free from alcohol and drugs will produce extra time. Use it to develop the new man. It's imperative for you to follow the exhortation of Jesus, "So I say to you, ask, and it will be given to you; seek, and you will find; knock, and it will be opened to you" (Luke 11:9).

As you live in obedience to God, you will experience His workings in various situations and circumstances to assist you in arriving at your destination. In your new walk, always keep in mind; He is the sovereign God over all, who will indeed fulfill His every promise.

And we know that God causes all things to work together for good to those who love God, to those who are called according to His purpose. For those whom He foreknew, He also predestined to become conformed to the image of His Son, so that He would be the firstborn among many brethren; and these whom He predestined, He also called; and these whom He called, He also justified; and these whom He justified, He also glorified (Romans 8:28).

With God's help you will find, discover, and experience victory. Learn to hold on to the altar of God's grace and mercy. Claim God's word and stand steadfast upon His every promise. Victory will be discovered, experienced, and cherished as you follow God's Addiction Recovery Plan on The Biblical Path to Freedom.

> The thief comes only to steal and kill and
> destroy; I came that they might have life, and
> have it more abundantly (John 10:10).

Ten Biblical Steps to freedom

FREEDOM STEP ONE

I must acknowledge I am a sinner in need of deliverance from my sinful nature and behavior. Romans 3:23; 1 John 1:8; Romans 5:12

FREEDOM STEP TWO

I must understand Jesus Christ paid the penalty for my sin and offers me a new life.
Romans 5:8; John 3:16; 2 Corinthians 5:21

FREEDOM STEP THREE

I must understand salvation is a free gift and requires a heart decision on my part.
Romans 6:23; Ephesians 2:8-9; Revelation 3:20

FREEDOM STEP FOUR

I must repent and receive Jesus Christ as my personal Lord and Savior by faith.
Acts 3:19; 2 Peter 3:9; Romans 10:9

FREEDOM STEP FIVE

I must accept by faith the assurance of a new birth, and understand I am a new creature with a divine nature. John 3:3; 2 Corinthians 5:17; 2 Peter 1:4

FREEDOM STEP SIX

I must understand Jesus Christ has set me free and given me the power to live a clean life.
John 8:36; Romans 8:11; Ephesians 3:20

FREEDOM STEP SEVEN

I must turn over and surrender control of my life to Jesus Christ by letting go of my own ambitions, dreams, and desires. Matthew 16:25; John 12:25; Mark 8:34

FREEDOM STEP EIGHT

I must set aside the old life and put on the new life I have been given in Jesus Christ.

Ephesians 4:21-24; James 4:7; Colossians 3:10

FREEDOM STEP NINE

I must separate myself from people and places threatening to drag me back into the old lifestyle.

2 Corinthians 6:17; Psalm 1:1; 1 Peter 1:15

FREEDOM STEP TEN

I must share my new life with others and lead them toward the knowledge of Christ.

Matthew 28:19-20; Mark 5:19; Acts 1:8

Works Cited

Holy Bible: New American Standard Bible, Grand Rapids, Michigan, Zondervan Publishing House, 2000.

Holy Bible: King James Version, Nashville, Tennessee, Thomas Nelson, Inc. 1976.

54469512R00089

Made in the USA
Columbia, SC
31 March 2019